SEWING

Felicity Everett and Carol Garbera
Illustrated by Sara Silcock and Christine Berrington

Designed by Camilla Luff
Edited by Angela Wilkes

Cover design by Amanda Barlow. Cover photography by John Bellenis.

CONTENTS

2   About sewing
3   Things you need
4   Your sewing machine
6   Making the patterns
8   Getting ready
9   Cutting out
10 Making seams and darts
12 Cotton vest
16 Tee-shirt
20 Sweatshirt
24 Jeans
28 Gathered skirt
32 Baggy shirt
38 Jumpsuit
42 Basic hand sewing
44 Choosing fabric and thread
46 Taking your measurements
47 Understanding patterns
48 Lengthening or shortening
    patterns

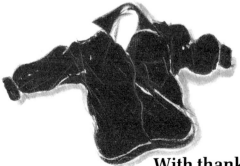

With thanks to John Garbera & Bill Le Fever

About sewing

Making your own clothes is enjoyable and a lot easier than you might think. It gives you a wide range of styles and fabrics to choose from and is cheaper than buying things ready made. This book gives you patterns for a colourful range of co-ordinated clothes you will want to make and wear, and shows you step-by-step how to make them. Some of the patterns are simple and others more difficult, but they are all easy to follow. The book covers all the basic dressmaking skills you need to know, from start to finish, and also tells you how to make your own patterns.

The patterns

The patterns in part one are designed to fit sizes 10 and 12. Each pattern is printed on a chart at the end of the sewing instructions. Follow the black outline for size 10 and the red one for size 12. You can find out how to draw the patterns to scale on pages 6 and 7. There are diagrams for suggested fabric layouts next to the patterns. All the layouts are for fabrics with naps.

Things you need

Your sewing machine

You need a sewing machine to make the clothes. Turn to pages 4 and 5 to find out more about sewing machines and how to thread them.

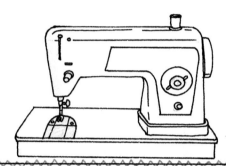

For making the patterns

Here are the things you need to make your own patterns. You can find out what to do on pages 6 and 7.

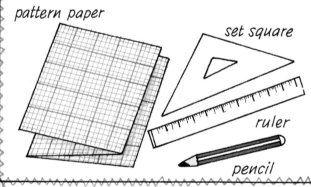

pattern paper

set square

ruler

pencil

For pressing

An iron and ironing board are almost as important as your sewing machine when you are making clothes. You can find out why on page 11.

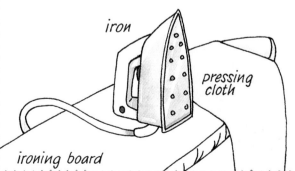

iron

pressing cloth

ironing board

Your sewing box

These are the general things you need for dressmaking. You can buy them in the haberdashery departments of large stores. Keep the dressmaking scissors for cutting fabric and make sure your pins and needles do not get rusty.

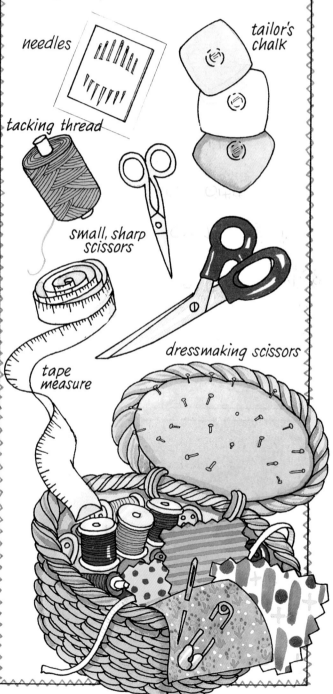

needles

tailor's chalk

tacking thread

small, sharp scissors

tape measure

dressmaking scissors

Your sewing machine

You need a sewing machine to make the clothes in this book. Electric machines are faster, but a hand machine will do. Put your machine on a table in a well-lit room or near a bright lamp.

Your machine may not look exactly the same as the one shown here. Check your machine handbook if you are not sure where things are. Try your machine out on scraps of fabric before you make anything.

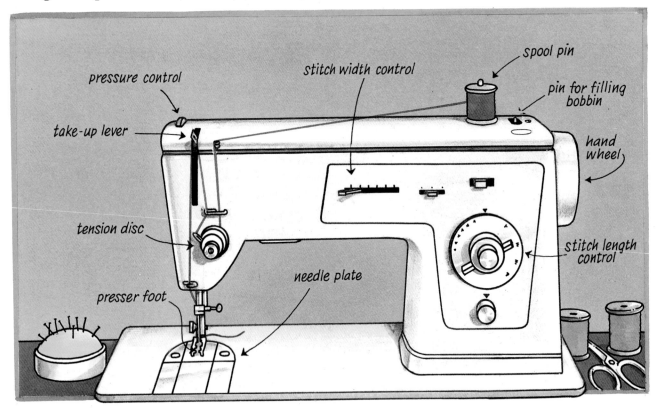

Filling the bobbin

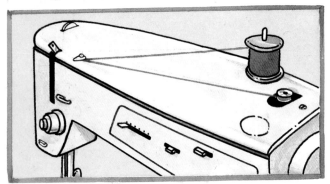

Put a reel of thread and the empty bobbin on the machine as shown. Pass the end of the thread round the clip and wind it a few times round the bobbin. Loosen the handwheel, work the machine until the bobbin is full and then cut the thread. Tighten the handwheel.

Threading the bobbin case

1. Slot the bobbin into the case as shown. Keep the end of the thread free of the case.

2. Pull the thread down the groove and under the clip.

3. Open the bobbin case handle and slot the case into position under the needle plate.

Check your machine handbook to find out what to do if your machine has a built-in bobbin case.

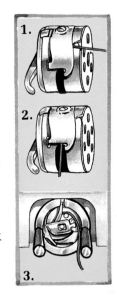

Threading the machine

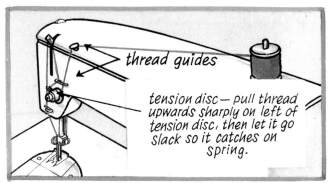

thread guides

tension disc — pull thread upwards sharply on left of tension disc, then let it go slack so it catches on spring.

Raise the presser foot. Put the reel of thread on the spool pin and guide the thread around the loops as shown in the picture. Thread the needle from left to right or from front to back, depending on the type of machine.

Raising the bobbin thread

1. Hold the top thread in your left hand and slowly turn the handwheel with your right until the needle picks up a loop of thread from the bottom bobbin.

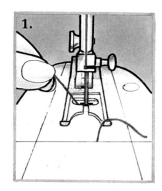

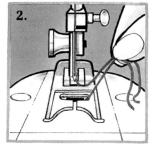

2. Gently pull both threads out and push them under the presser foot. Leave ends about 10cm long.

Tension

The tension is the amount of 'give' in the thread. If the thread is too tight, the seam puckers. If it is too slack, the stitches are loopy. The tension is right when the stitches form in the middle of the fabric.

tension too tight

tension too loose

tension correct

You can adjust the tension by turning the tension disc on the machine. Different fabrics need different tension. Check it on scraps of fabric until it is right.

Needle sizes

Sizes range from 9 (finest) to 18 (thickest). Use special ball-point needles for sewing jersey fabrics. A sharp point may divide the strand of yarn and spoil the fabric. The lighter the fabric, the finer the needle you should use. Use size 11 or 14 for medium-weight fabrics.

Pressure

Some machines have a pressure control which helps to feed the fabric evenly through the machine. The thinner the fabric, the lighter the pressure needed.

Stitches

You can alter the stitch length or width by adjusting the controls on the machine (see picture on facing page).

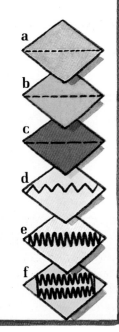

a For running stitch, set stitch width control at 0.

b A medium stitch length is suitable for most fabrics.

c Use the longest stitch length for gathering.

d,e Use zig zag stitches for sewing stretch fabrics. You have to adjust both the stitch length and width for these.

f When you are sewing buttonholes, use the shortest stitch length and a wide stitch width.

Making the patterns

The patterns in part one are printed in chart form on grids. Here you can find out how to scale them up on to pattern paper to make your own patterns. It is much easier than you might think.

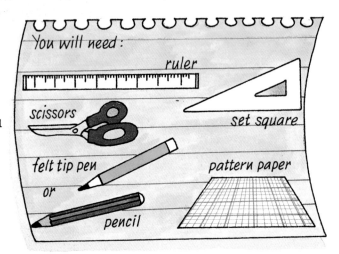

Pattern paper

You can buy special paper for making your own patterns in the haberdashery sections of fabric shops and department stores. It looks like grid paper marked into 1cm and 5cm squares. If you cannot buy the paper you can make your own. You will need large sheets of brown paper, a pencil, a ruler and a set square.

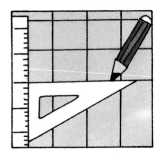

First divide your paper into 5cm squares. Rule lengthwise lines first, then crosswise ones, using a set square to make sure they cross at right angles.

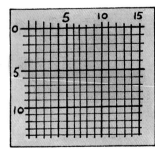

Divide each big square into 25 1cm squares, then mark every fifth square down the side and across the top, as shown, starting in the top left corner.

Things to remember

The scale of the charts to the patterns is 1 to 5. This means that a 1cm square on the chart = a 5cm square on the pattern paper. A 2mm square on the chart = a 1cm square on the pattern paper.

There are outlines for sizes 10 and 12 on each pattern. Size 10 is outlined in black and size 12 in red. Make sure you copy out the right outline for your size.

The symbols on the patterns are called construction marks. You can find out what they mean on the opposite page. You use tailor tacks to mark them on the fabric (see page 9).

Making a pattern

Collect everything you need before you start. If your pattern paper is creased, iron it with a cool iron, then spread it out on a table or on the floor.

Draw the big pattern pieces first. Mark crosses on the paper where the widest and longest points of each piece come. Draw a box through them.

Using the big squares as a rough guide and the small ones to fix the exact position, draw crosses where the pattern piece meets the box.

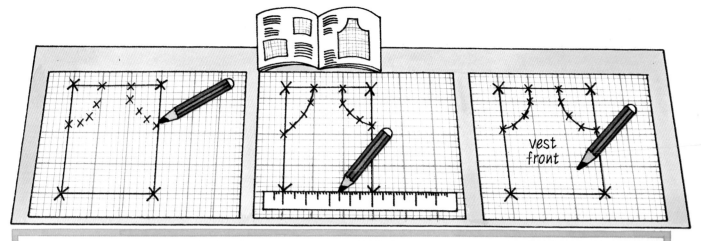

Plot the precise outline of the piece by making a cross at each point where the outline of the pattern piece crosses the grid lines of the paper.

Using a ruler for the straight lines, join the centres of the crosses together to make an even cutting line. Draw the curves carefully and slowly.

Check the number of big squares on your pattern against the number of squares on the chart. Write the name of the pattern piece on it.

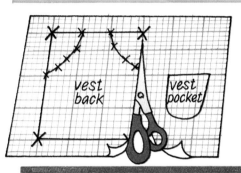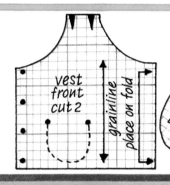

Draw the rest of the pattern pieces in the same way, fitting the smaller pattern pieces between the big pieces. Then cut them all out.

Copy everything that is on the pattern chart on to your pattern pieces, including the number of times you should cut out each piece.

Give each pattern piece a letter (so you know if you lose one) then put them in an envelope and write the name of the pattern on the front.

Construction marks

Notches help you match one piece of a garment to another, e.g. a collar to a shirt.

You use dots to match seamlines when joining two pieces of a garment together and to mark pocket positions.

Darts look like this. You can find out how to stitch them on page 11.

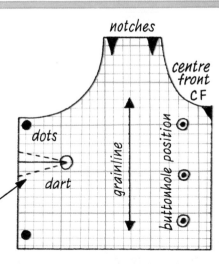

The centre front and centre back of a pattern are often marked to help you position other pattern pieces in line with them.

Always line the grainline up with the straight grain of the fabric – parallel to the selvedges.

Pattern pieces which are to be placed on a fold have arrows to show which edge goes on the fold.

7

Getting ready

When you are making clothes it is worth taking the time to prepare and cut out the fabric carefully, so that your clothes hang well. If you cut out the fabric in a hurry it is very easy to make expensive mistakes. Below you can find out how to start.

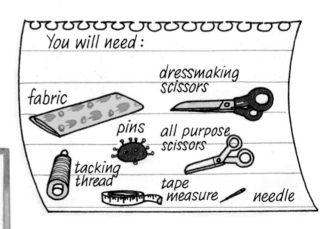

You will need: fabric, dressmaking scissors, pins, all purpose scissors, tacking thread, tape measure, needle

Preparing the pattern pieces

Patterns from shops give you all the pieces on big sheets of paper. You have to cut them out roughly before you can pin them down. Smooth out the pattern paper with a warm iron if it is creased.

Preparing the fabric

If your fabric is creased, press it well. Stretchy fabrics should be left spread out overnight so they can 'relax'.

If you are using cotton, or another fabric which might shrink, it is a good idea to wash and iron it before you lay it out.

If your fabric has not been cut off the roll in a straight line, straighten the edge as follows.

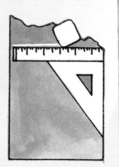

Put a set square flat along the selvedge and hold a ruler along the top, as shown. Draw a chalk line across the fabric and cut along it.

Fabrics with a nap

For a fabric with a nap or a one-way design, you must lay out all the pattern pieces with the nap or pattern facing the same way. If the pattern layout shows a widthways fold, cut along the fold, then lay the two pieces of fabric wrong sides together, making sure that the nap or pattern runs the same way on both pieces.

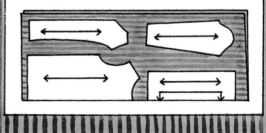

Understanding the pattern layout

All patterns give recommended pattern layouts. In this book they are on the same page as the pattern.

There is usually a different layout for each fabric width. The layout shows you where to fold the fabric and put each pattern piece.

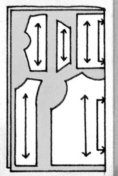

Checks and stripes

Avoid checks and stripes if you are a beginner as they have to match at all seams and this is difficult to do. If you want to use a striped or checked fabric, choose a simple pattern and remember to match seams on the seamline, not the cutting line.

Cutting out

Fold the fabric and arrange the pattern pieces as shown on your layout. Make sure they all fit before you pin them down. For a napped fabric, see opposite page.

If a pattern piece says 'cut 2 to pair', cut it out once, then turn the pattern piece over and cut it out again, so you have a right and a left piece.

Position each piece so the grainline runs along the straight grain of the fabric*. Measure from the selvedge to make sure it is straight.

Pin the grainline in position first, then smooth the pattern outwards and pin round the edges. Put the pins in at right angles to the pattern piece.

Before you start cutting out, make sure that you have not missed out any pattern pieces and check the right ones are on the double layer of fabric.

Cut each piece out carefully. When you come to a notch, cut it outwards instead of into the seam allowance. Cut double and triple notches in a block.

Leave the pattern pinned to the fabric until you have transferred the dots on to the fabric using tailor tacks. You can see how to do this below.

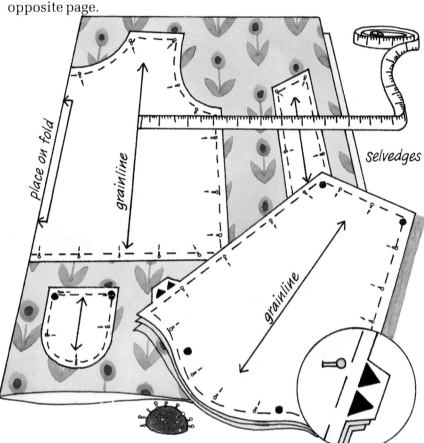

place on fold · *grainline* · *grainline* · *selvedges* · *notches*

Making tailor tacks

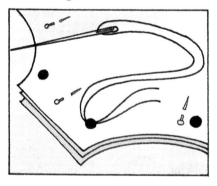

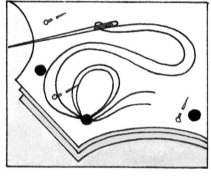

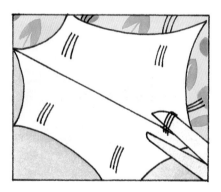

With a double length of unknotted thread, stitch through the pattern and both layers of fabric. Leave ends about 2.5cm long.

Backstitch in the same place to make a loop. Cut the thread about 2.5cm from the fabric, as shown. Cut the loop and lift the pattern away from the fabric.

Gently separate the two layers of fabric and cut the threads in between to leave a few tufts of thread in each piece. These are your tailor tacks.

* See page 45

Making seams and darts

As clothes are held together by seams, you must make them strong and neaten the raw edges so they do not fray. There are different kinds of seam, but the type shown below is the one you will need to use most often.

Darts are used to give shape and fullness to clothes. The clothes in this book do not have darts, but it is useful to know how to make them.

The seam allowance

The seam allowance is the distance between the edge of the fabric and the seamline (the line you stitch along). Your pattern tells you what the seam allowance is. You will find it easier to sew straight along the seamline if you line up the edge of your fabric with one of the grooves in the needle plate of your machine.

Pinning

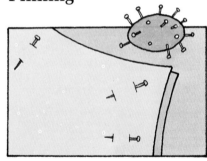

Always use clean, sharp pins. Blunt, rusty ones make holes in the fabric. Pin the edges of the fabric together, putting the pins in at right angles to the edge.

Tacking

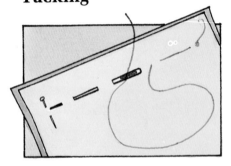

Starting with a knot or a couple of stitches, tack close to the seamline. Take the pins out as you tack, and finish off with a single backstitch.

Machining

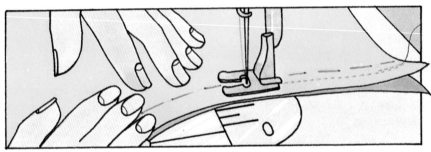

Check that your sewing machine has the right size needle in it and is set to the right tension and pressure. Try the stitching on a scrap of fabric.

Check the seam allowance and put the needle in on the seamline. Backstitch at the beginning and stitch along the seamline. Backstitch at the end.

Neatening Seams

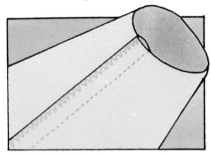

If the seam allowance is narrow, machine the raw edges together with a short, wide zigzag. Press the seam towards the back or body of the garment.

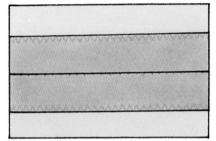

For a wider seam allowance, zigzag stitch each edge separately or oversew them by hand (see p. 42), then press them apart.

For firmly woven fabric which does not fray easily you can neaten the raw edges by trimming them with pinking shears to give a zigzag edge.

Darts

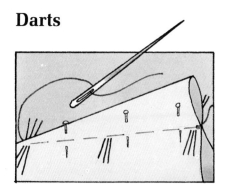
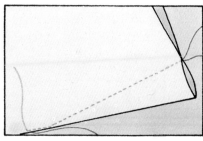
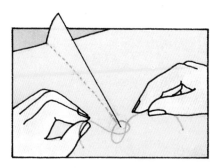

Mark the position of the dart with tailor tacks (see page 9). Fold and pin it as shown, then tack it from the wide edge to the point and take out the pins.

Stitch from wide edge to the point. Make the last few stitches right on the edge of the fold, so that the dart lies flat on the right side of the fabric.

Tie the ends of the thread in a knot to secure your stitching (backstitching makes the point of the dart too bulky). Press the dart to one side.

Pressing

When you are sewing, you should press each piece of stitching you do, especially seams and darts, to make sure they lie flat. Put the ironing board up before you start sewing, so you can press things as you go along.

Before you press your sewing, take out the pins and tacking. Test the heat of the iron on a spare piece of the fabric.

A steam iron is best for pressing. If you do not have one, use a damp cloth, especially for thick fabrics such as wool and tweed and fabrics which crease badly, such as linen. It is best to press things on the wrong side.

Temperature guide

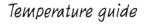 hot iron (cotton, linen, viscose)

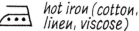 warm iron (polyester, mixtures, wool)

cool iron (synthetics)

do not iron

Use the tip of the iron to open up seams and get into the corners. Press curved seams on the end of your ironing board with the tip of your iron.

Pressing is not the same as ironing. Gently lower the iron on to the area to be pressed and then lift it off again. Do not slide it across the fabric.

Cotton vest

This vest is the easiest thing in the book to make. It is a clingy style which looks best made in jersey fabric.

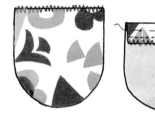

You will need:
60-70 cm of 115/150 cm
wide jersey fabric
1 reel of matching sewing
thread
ballpoint sewing needles

Sizes

To fit chest: 83/87cm
Finished size
chest: 85/90cm
length: 56/59cm

Sewing jersey

Try not to stretch the fabric as you are stitching it.

Use a medium ballpoint needle*

Stitch seams with a short, narrow zigzag stitch.

Make the pattern, following the chart on page 15, and cut it out. Then cut out the fabric.

Suggested fabrics

Cotton jersey, stretch towelling, silky jersey.

Pocket

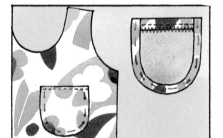

Neaten the top edge of the pocket with a short, wide zigzag stitch. Turn in 1.5cm along the top. Tack and press. Stitch close to neatened edge**

Turn in 5mm round rest of pocket. Tack and press. Pin the pocket on vest front so its top edge lines up with tailor tacks on front. Tack. Topstitch.

Topstitching

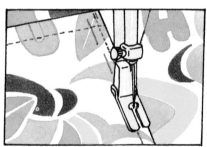

Position the presser foot of machine so the stitching comes 1-2mm from the edge of the pocket. Stitch round pocket, leaving top edge free.

* See page 5   ** Set stitch width control at 0 for running stitch.

Shoulder and side seams

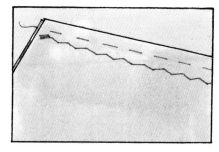

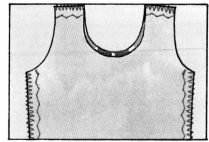

Pin front and back of vest together at shoulder and side seams, with right sides together. Tack in place, taking pins out as you go.

Set the zigzag on your sewing machine to a medium length, narrow width setting. Stitch the seams. Backstitch at start and finish.

Change the stitch setting back to the short, wide zigzag you used for the top edge of the pocket and stitch the seam edges together to neaten them.

Finishing the neck and sleeves

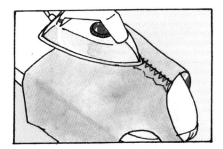

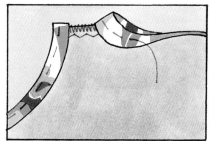

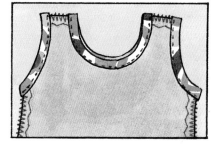

Take out the tacking stitches. Using a warm iron, press the neatened edges of the seams towards the back of the vest along the seamline.

Turn in 5mm round the neck and armholes. Tack and press. Turn in another 1cm to cover the raw edges. Tack and press in place.

With your machine set at a medium stitch length, straight stitch round the neck and sleeve openings about 2mm from the inner folded edge.

Hemming

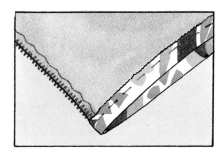

Turn in 5mm round the bottom edge of the vest, as you did to finish the armholes and neck. Tack and press turning in place, as shown.

Measure 1.5cm in from the first turning and make a second one. Tack and press. Stitch it in place about 2mm in from the inner folded edge.

13

Appliqué vest

Here you can find out how to sew a letter or number on your vest.

You will need

60-70cm of fabric as for vest
piece of contrast colour fabric (cotton, satin or poplin) 25cm × 25cm
piece of graph paper 25cm × 25cm
piece of iron-on interfacing 25cm × 25cm
all the other things you need for the vest (see p. 12)

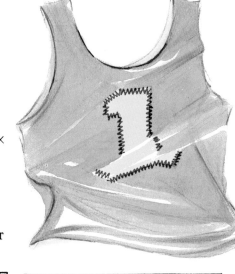

You must sew the letter on to the front of the vest before you sew the front and back together.

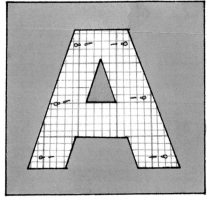

On the graph paper draw a letter about 20cm square, no part of it narrower than 4cm.

Cut out the letter and pin it on to the fabric. Draw round it and cut it out carefully.

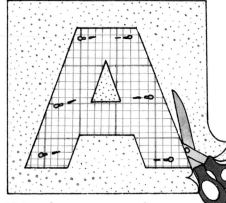

Using the same paper letter as your pattern, cut out an identical piece of interfacing.

Iron the interfacing * on to the wrong side of the fabric and tack the letter on to the vest.

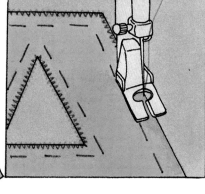

Stitch round the letter, using a short, wide zigzag so that all the raw edges are covered.

Make the vest, following the method on pages 12 and 13.

Mini dress

You can adapt the vest pattern to make a mini dress. It is cut straight, so make sure that the finished chest measurement is the same size or bigger than your hip measurement.

You will need

1m of 115cm or 150cm wide jersey fabric
all the other things you need for the vest (see p. 12)

Sizes

To fit chest: 83/87cm
Finished size:
chest: 85/90cm
length: 85cm

Method

Follow the basic vest pattern, but add 29cm to the length (this includes the hem).

Make up as for vest, following the method on pages 12 and 13.

Vest pattern

The seam allowance is 1cm throughout.

Layout for fabric 150cm wide

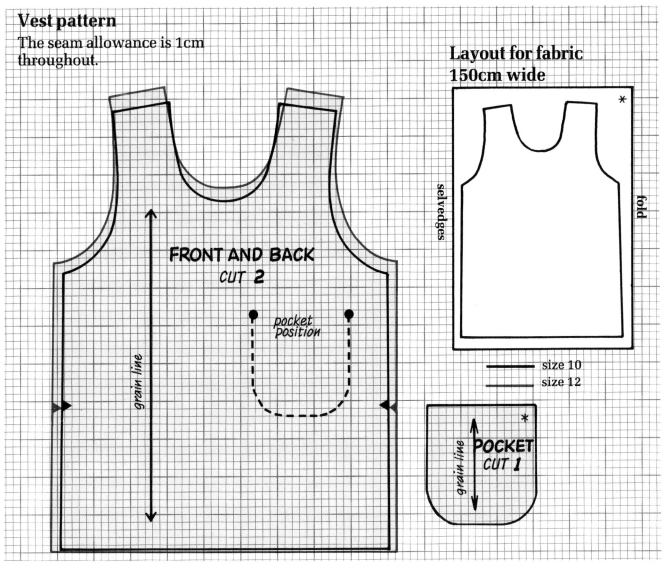

FRONT AND BACK
CUT 2

pocket position

grain line

selvedges

fold

—— size 10
—— size 12

POCKET
CUT 1

grain line

* you can fit the pocket piece in to the right of the armhole when the fabric is unfolded.

Tee-shirt

You can make this simple tee shirt from almost any fabric (see below). You can make a short or long sleeved version and on page 18 you can find out how to make a mini tee-shirt.

on page 18 you can find out how to make a mini tee-shirt.

You will need:

Long-sleeved tee-shirt:
2m 30 of 90cm wide fabric
OR 1m 20 of 115/150 cm wide fabric

Short-sleeved tee-shirt:
1m 70 of 90cm wide fabric
OR 90cm of 115/150 cm wide fabric

For both versions:
1 reel of matching sewing thread
1 m of 16 mm wide bias binding in matching colour (or white)

Sizes

To fit chest: 83/87cm
Finished size
chest: 106/110cm
length: 56/58cm
long sleeve length: 47cm
short sleeve length: 15cm

Method

Make the tee-shirt pattern, following the chart on page 19 and cut it out. Then cut out the fabric.

following the chart on page 19

Sewing jersey

If you are using jersey fabric to make the tee-shirt, remember to use zigzag stitch for all seams as for the vest on pages 12 and 13.

as for the vest on pages 12 and 13.

Suggested fabrics

Cotton jersey, stretch towelling, fine cotton, brushed cotton, Viyella, needlecord, satin.

Pocket

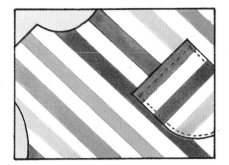

Hem top and sides of pockets as for vest pocket (see page 12). Tack in line with tailor tacks on front. Topstitch in place.

Shoulder seams

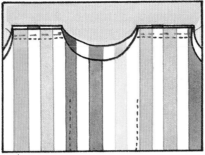

With right sides facing, pin the front and back of the tee-shirt together at shoulder seams and tack them in place.

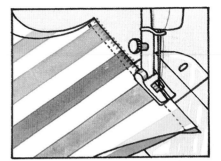

Take out pins and stitch seams. Neaten raw edges together, using zigzag stitch and press towards back of tee-shirt.

Sewing in sleeves

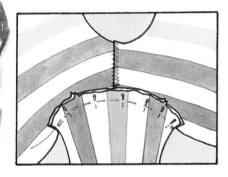

With right sides facing, pin sleeves into armholes, matching the notches. Tack in place, then take out pins.

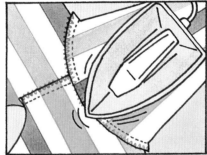

Stitch carefully, stretching fabric round lower armhole curves. Zigzag raw edges together and press inwards.

What is bias binding?

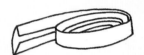

Bias binding is a kind of tape which is cut on the bias of the fabric (see page 45). This makes it stretchy and easy to bind round curved edges. It has a small, pressed hem along each edge.

Binding the neck

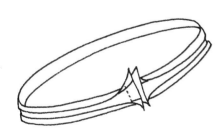

Cut a piece of bias binding 57/58cm long. With right sides facing, stitch the ends together to make a circle.

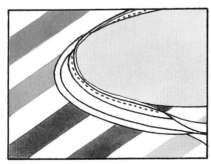

Pin right sides of binding to right side of neck so raw edges match. Tack. Stitch close to top fold in binding, as shown.

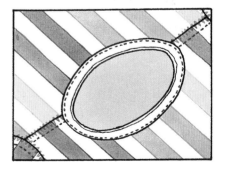

Press binding to wrong side of neck so seam is on the edge. Tack in place. Stitch close to fold in binding, as shown.

Underarm and side seams

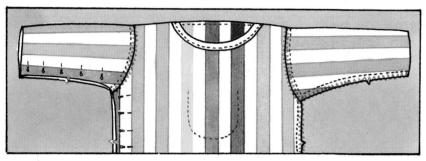

With right sides facing and matching notches, pin front to back at underarm sleeve and side seams.

Tack, then take out pins and stitch seams. Neaten raw edges together with zig zag stitch and press them towards back.

Hemming and finishing

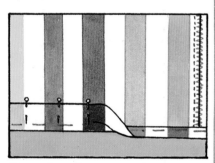

To make a hem, turn in 5mm round bottom of tee-shirt. Tack and press. Turn in another 2cm. Pin, tack and press. Stitch close to inner fold.

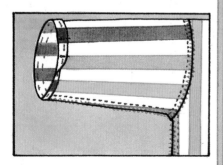

Hem sleeves in the same way, but make the second turnings 1cm deep. Turn tee-shirt the right way out and press*.

Mini Tee-shirt

You can adapt the tee-shirt pattern to make a mini version.

You will need

1m 60 of 92cm wide fabric
80cm of 115/150cm wide fabric
All the other things you need for the tee-shirt (see page 16).

Sizes

To fit chest: 83/87cm
Finished length: 39/41cm

Method

Make the pattern for short-sleeved tee-shirt, but cut along the mini tee-shirt cutting line. Make up as for tee-shirt **, following the method on pp. 17-18.

Applique Tee-shirt

Make an appliqué letter or number (see page 14) and stitch on to front of tee-shirt. Make up as for tee-shirt, following the method on pp. 17-18.

* Hem sleeves in the same way for short or long sleeves.
    ** The mini tee shirt has no pocket.

Tee-shirt pattern

Layout for fabric 115cm or 150cm wide

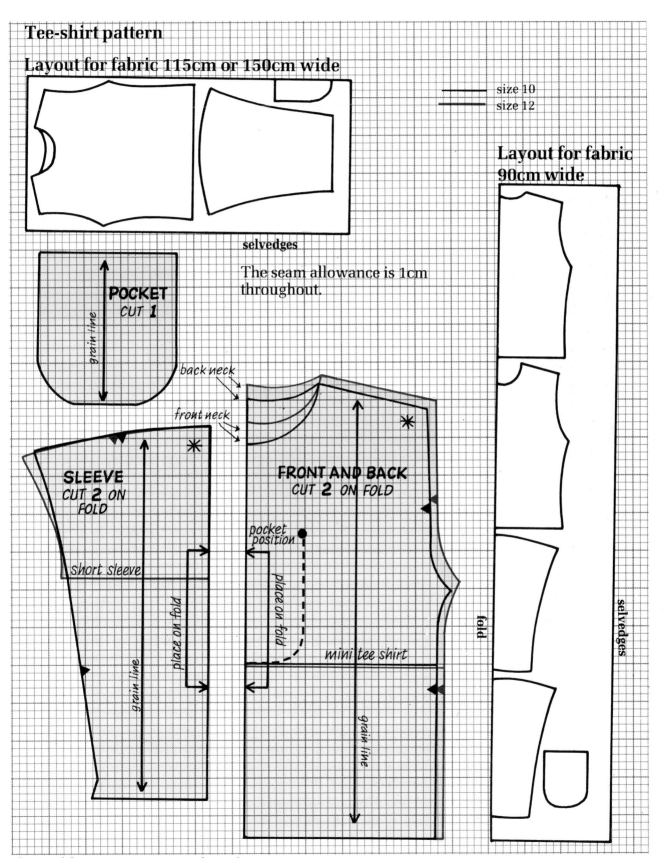

size 10

size 12

selvedges

Layout for fabric 90cm wide

The seam allowance is 1cm throughout.

POCKET CUT *1*

grain line

back neck

front neck

SLEEVE CUT *2* ON FOLD

short sleeve

place on fold

grain line

pocket position

place on fold

FRONT AND BACK CUT *2* ON FOLD

mini tee shirt

place on fold

grain line

fold

selvedges

*If using fabric 115 or 150 cm wide, make pattern pieces for the complete front, back and sleeve by cutting them out on folded paper.

Sweatshirt

You will need
1 m 20/ 1 m 30 of
150 cm wide fabric
40 cm of matching
tubular knit ribbing at
least 60 cm wide (when flat)
ballpoint sewing needles
1 reel of matching
sewing thread

This sweatshirt is easier to make than you might think. It is the ribbing that makes it look professional and you can buy it from most department stores and fabric shops. If you cannot find the colour you want, buy white ribbing and dye it.

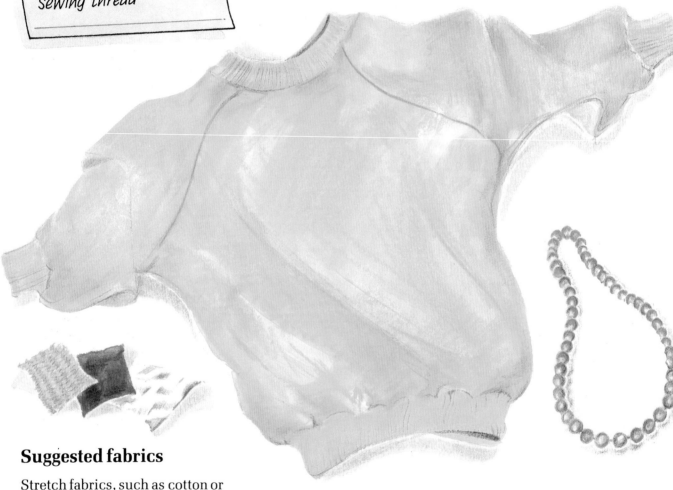

Suggested fabrics

Stretch fabrics, such as cotton or cotton/acrylic mix sweatshirt fabric, stretch towelling, heavy knit jersey*

Sizes

To fit chest: 83/87cm
Finished size
chest: 102/108cm
length: 59.5/62.5cm
underarm sleeve length: 46/47cm

Method

Make the sweatshirt pattern following the chart on page 37 and cut the following pieces from the sweatshirt ribbing:

Hipband: 2 pieces 15cm × 28cm
Cuffs: 2 pieces 15cm × 18cm
Neck: 1 piece 7.5cm × 43cm

* remember to sew jersey fabric with zigzag stitch (see page 12).

Different kinds of sleeve

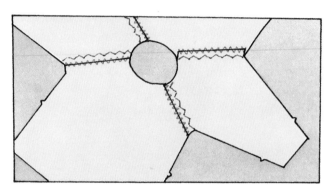

raglan sleeves   set-in sleeves

Raglan sleeves are different from 'set-in' sleeves. They join on to the neck, rather than the shoulder whereas set-in sleeves are stitched into the armhole of a garment.

Stitch with a medium, narrow zigzag stitch (use throughout for stitching seams). Neaten raw edges together with a short, wide zigzag stitch and press towards body of sweatshirt.

Hipband

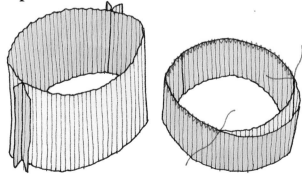

With right sides of hipband ribbing facing, tack side seams. Stitch, turning right sides out, and fold in half lengthwise to make a tube. Zigzag stitch raw edges together loosely.

Joining sleeves to armholes

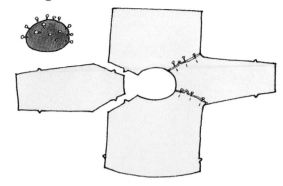

With right sides together, pin the raglan sleeves to the front and back of the sweatshirt along the shoulder seams, as shown. Tack in place.

Underarm and side seams

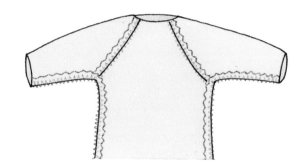

Pin side seams and underarm sleeve seams together. Tack. Stitch, stretching fabric gently round the underarm curves. Neaten raw edges together and press towards back.

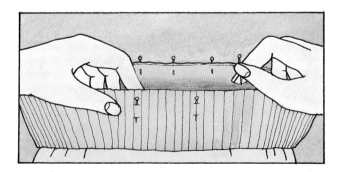

Place right side of the ribbing tube against right side of the sweatshirt, matching side seams, and pin evenly around the hem, stretching the ribbing to fit. Tack in place.

Cuffs

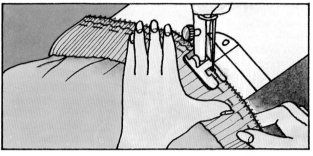
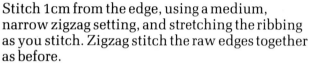
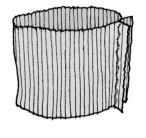
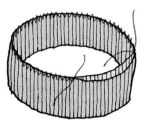

Stitch 1cm from the edge, using a medium, narrow zigzag setting, and stretching the ribbing as you stitch. Zigzag stitch the raw edges together as before.

Fold each cuff in half widthwise and stitch the short ends together with right sides facing. Turn right sides out and fold lengthwise as for hipband. Tack. Zigzag raw edges together.

Short sleeved sweatshirt

This short-sleeved sweatshirt makes a cool and casual summer top.

You will need

1m/1m 10 of 150cm wide fabric
40cm of ribbing
all the other things you need for the sweatshirt (see page 20)

Method

When making your pattern, cut off sleeves at short sleeve line. Cut 2 cuff ribs 8cm × 26cm. Make up cuff and stitch on to sleeve as for sweatshirt (see pp. 20 and 21).

Loose, baggy top

You can adapt the pattern to make this top without ribbing. Instead of sewing ribbing to the cuffs, neck and hipband, neatly stitch along the raw edges using a short, wide zigzag stitch. The fabric will curl up with wear and cover the stitching.

loose, baggy top

short sleeved sweatshirt

Neckband

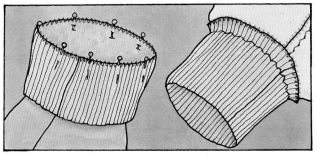

Pin cuffs to right sides of sleeves, as shown. Match seams and stretch ribbing to fit. Tack and stitch. Zigzag raw edges together to neaten them.

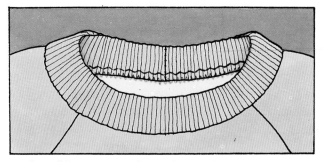

Make ribbing into tube as for cuffs. Match seam to centre back of sweatshirt and pin ribbing evenly around neck. Tack, stitch and neaten as before, then press lightly.

Sweatshirt pattern

The seam allowance is 1cm throughout.

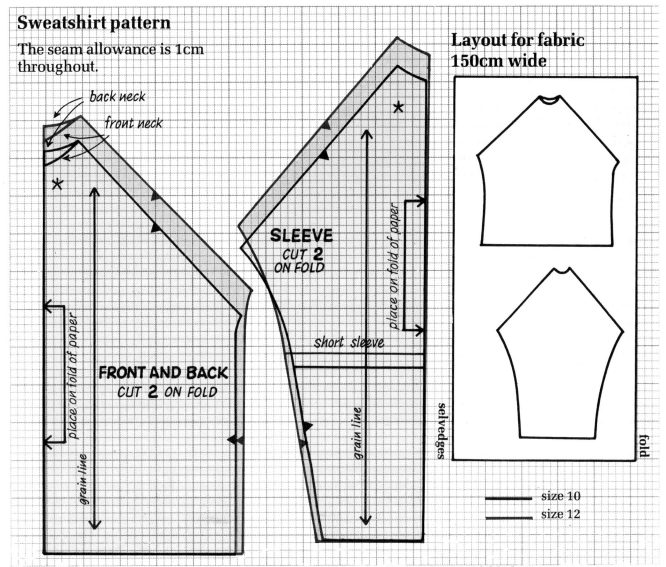

*Make pattern pieces for the complete back, front and sleeve by cutting them on folded paper.

Jeans

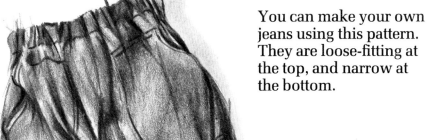

You can make your own jeans using this pattern. They are loose-fitting at the top, and narrow at the bottom.

Suggested fabrics

Cottons: poplin, drill, crinkle cotton, denim, needlecord.

Sizes

To fit hips: 88/92cm
waist: 64/74cm
Finished size
hips: 96/102cm
length: 102/106cm
inside leg length: 73/75cm

Method

Make the pattern following the chart on pages 26 and 27 and cut it out. Then cut out the fabric.

How to double topstitch seams

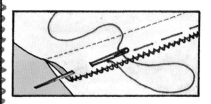

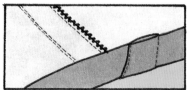

On the wrong side of the garment, tack down the neatened edge of the seam allowance through all layers of fabric. Then turn garment the right way out.

Do two lines of topstitching — one next to the seam, just inside the seam allowance, and the other about 6mm away (next to zigzag edge on wrong side of fabric).

Crutch seams

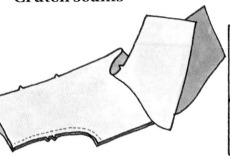

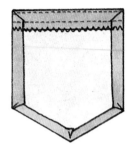

With right sides facing, tack two trouser fronts together along the crutch seam (curved seam between top of inside leg and waist). Stitch.

Neaten raw edges together. Press to right of seam. Double topstitch (see opposite page). Do the back crutch seam in the same way.

Back pockets

Neaten top edges of back pockets. Press 1.5cm to wrong side. Double topstitch. Press 1cm to wrong side round three remaining edges.

Front pockets

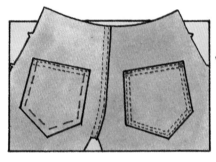

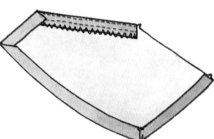

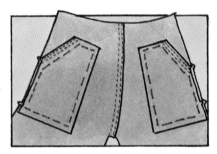

Line pockets up with tacks on back of trousers. Tack. Double topstitch round unstitched sides of pockets. Leave the tops open.

Neaten sloping edges of front pockets, as for tops of back pockets. Turn in 1cm to wrong side at top, bottom and long side of front pockets. Press.

Tack the pockets in line with tailor tacks on front of trousers, matching notches so that raw edges of pockets match side edges of trousers.

Side seams

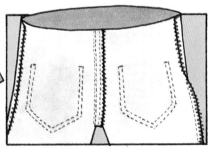

Inside leg seams

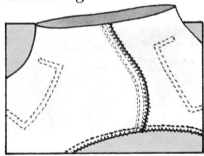

Double topstitch round top, long side and bottom of pockets. Stitch raw edges of pockets to edges of trousers, 5mm in.

With right sides facing, tack front to back of trousers at side seams. Stitch. Neaten seams and press towards back. Double topstitch.

With right sides of fabric facing, tack inside leg seams. Stitch. Neaten seams together and press them towards the back of trousers.

What is a casing?

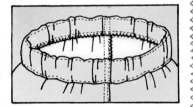

A casing is a tube of fabric threaded with elastic or cord. It makes a comfortable waistband which you can adjust to fit.

Waistband

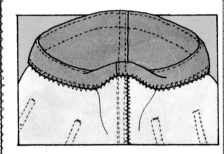

Zigzag waist edge of trousers and turn in 5cm. Press. Tack. Topstitch close to fold and again, 3.5cm lower down, leaving a 4cm gap at back seam.

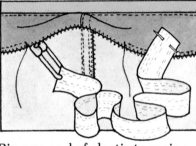

Pin one end of elastic to casing. Thread other end through with a big safety pin. Pin both ends together. Try on trousers and adjust elastic to fit.

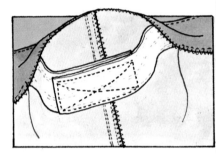

Stitch ends of elastic together being careful not to stitch it to casing at same time. Trim spare elastic 1cm from stitching. Topstitch 4cm gap in casing.

Hems

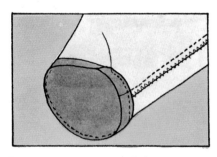

Turn in 5mm on each leg. Press. Turn in another 1cm to hide raw edges. Press and tack. Topstitch. Roll up hems to the length you want.

Jeans pattern

Layout for fabric 150cm wide

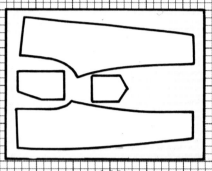

fold

The seam allowance is 1cm throughout.

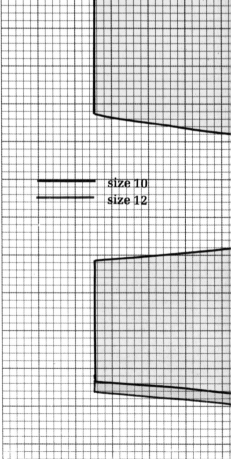

size 10
size 12

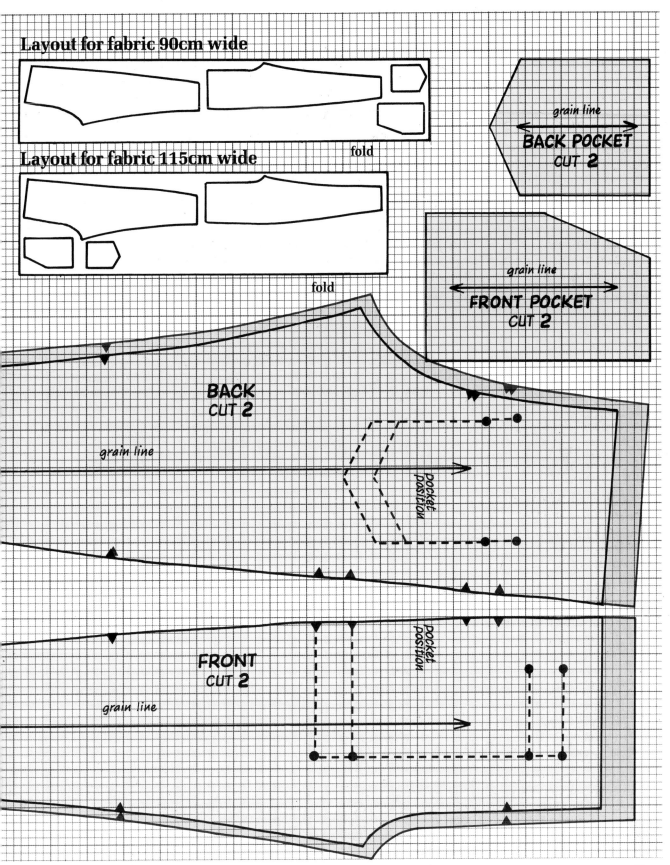

Layout for fabric 90cm wide

fold

Layout for fabric 115cm wide

fold

grain line

BACK POCKET
CUT **2**

grain line

FRONT POCKET
CUT **2**

BACK
CUT **2**

grain line

pocket position

FRONT
CUT **2**

grain line

pocket position

Gathered skirt

You do not need a pattern for this skirt. It is just made from two rectangles of fabric, a waistband and two pockets.

Sizes

To fit waist: 64/67cm
Finished size
length (including waistband): 84cm
width round hem: 224cm

Suggested fabrics

Cotton poplin, lawn, madras, seersucker, brushed cotton, Viyella, fine needlecord.

Method

Cut out the following widths of fabric, as shown in the pattern layout on p. 31.

2 widths 86cm deep for skirt
1 waistband, 10cm × 66/71cm
2 pockets, 21cm × 27cm

Interfacing

Cut 1 strip for the waistband, 5cm × 66/71cm.
Cut 2 strips 3cm × 21cm for the tops of the pockets.

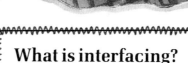
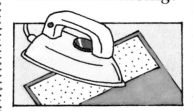

What is interfacing?

Interfacing is a special fabric you attach to the wrong side of fabric you want to stiffen. It comes in different weights. The iron-on kind is the easiest to use.

Attaching interfacing

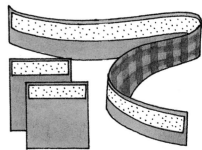

Iron the wrong side of the interfacing on to the wrong side of the tops of the pockets and lengthways on to one half of the waistband.

Pockets

Zigzag stitch top edges of pockets and turn in 3cm hems. Tack, press and stitch twice, as shown. Press 1cm hems around other 3 sides of pockets.

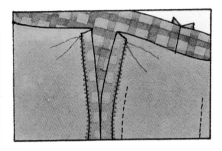

Tack pockets on to skirt front, 9cm below top edge and 3cm in from side edges. Topstitch around 3 sides of pockets about 2mm in from the edges.

Side seams

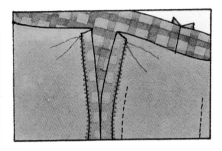

With right sides of skirt together, tack side seams. Leave a 21cm gap at top of left seam for zip. Stitch. Neaten seams with zigzag and press open.

Using a zip foot

A zip foot has a notch on each side so that you can stitch to the right or the left of the zip. Stitch both sides of the zip from the base upwards.

Stitch the right side of the zip first, with the zip foot to the left of the needle. Move the foot to the right of the needle to stitch the left side of the zip.

Zip

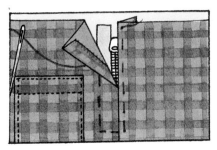

With skirt right sides out, put zip in opening, 1.5cm from top of skirt. Tack right side of zip so fabric almost meets teeth and left side so fabric covers teeth.

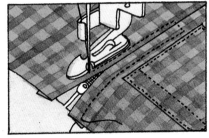

Using a zip foot, stitch zip into opening so that stitching comes close to edge of pocket on front of skirt and close to fold on back of skirt.

Gathers

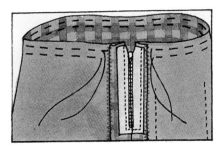

Set the machine to a long stitch length. Stitch twice round the top of the skirt, 5mm and 1.5cm below top edge. Leave long threads at beginning and end.

Gently pull ends of both threads to gather waist until it measures 61/66cm (each side should measure half this). Tie ends of threads together.

Waistband

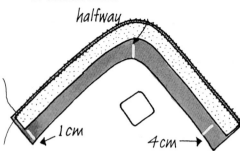

Zigzag along interfaced edge of waistband. Measure 1cm in from left end, 4cm from right end and halfway between the two and mark with chalk.

With right sides together, pin waistband to skirt, lining up chalk marks, as shown. Adjust gathers evenly between marks. Tack in place.

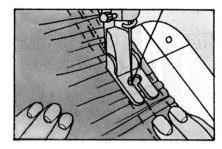

Stitch waistband to skirt with a 1cm seam allowance. Stitch between the rows of gathering. Take out the lower row of gathering stitches.

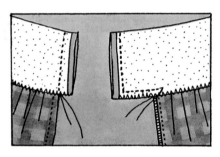

Fold waistband in half, right sides together, and tack each end so it is square. Stitch 1cm in. At end with overlap, stitch along lower edge as far as zip.

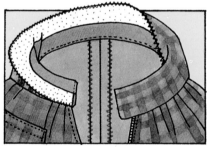

Trim corners of waistband and turn right way out. Ease out corners so you have neat, square edges. Press waistband in half to finished depth of 4cm.

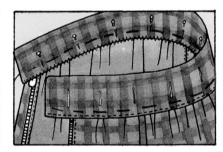

Pin neatened edge of waistband to wrong side of skirt, covering raw edges. Tack in place so it lies smoothly. Stitch along right side, close to seam.

Hem

Finishing

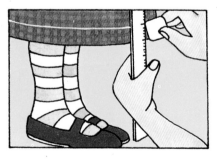

Try on skirt. Ask a friend to pin up hem to the length you want. For a 5cm hem*, turn up and press 5mm to wrong side. Turn up a further 4.5cm and tack.

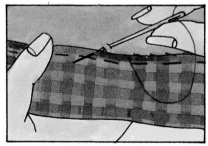

Hem neatly by hand (see page 43), making sure that the stitches do not show on the right side and that the stitching does not pucker.

Handsew or machine a 1cm horizontal buttonhole on front of waistband 1cm in from edge (see opposite). Sew a button on to overlapping flap.

* Whatever depth you want the hem to be, remember to allow 5mm for the first turning.

Machine stitched buttonholes

Attach buttonhole foot*. Mark buttonhole position. With short, wide zigzag work down one side of buttonhole on right side of garment.

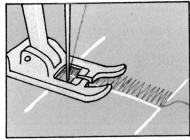

When you reach end marker, lift foot and turn fabric. Set stitch width to its widest and make a few stitches the width of whole buttonhole.

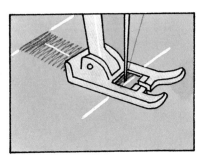

Re-set stitch width to its previous position. Stitch other side of buttonhole. Make a few stitches the width of buttonhole at end.

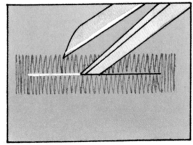

Tie loose threads together at back. Snip down middle of buttonhole, being careful not to cut any stitches.

Sewing on buttons

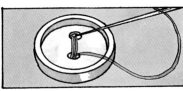

Sew through button

With a double length of knotted thread, stitch through button and fabric, keeping a small gap in between. Fasten off on wrong side.

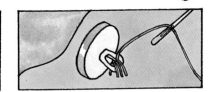

Shank button

Holding button at right angles to fabric, stitch through the hole in the shank and through the fabric. Fasten off securely.

* Look in your machine handbook to find out how.

Fabric layout for skirt

FRONT
CUT *1* ON FOLD

BACK
CUT *1* ON FOLD

WAISTBAND
CUT *1* ON FOLD

POCKET
CUT *2*

fold

Layout for fabric 115cm or 150cm wide

Baggy shirt

This loose-fitting shirt can look smart or casual, depending on the fabric you make it from. It is suitable for boys or girls.

Suggested fabrics

Fine cottons, lawn, voile, poplin, seersucker, brushed cotton, viyella.

Sizes

To fit chest: 83/87cm
Finished size chest: 118/122cm
back length: 72/74cm
(excluding collar)
underarm sleeve: 43/45cm
collar size: 36/39cm

Interfacing

From the interfacing, cut a collar piece, a neckband piece and 2 cuff pieces (half the width of the cuff). Trim off seam allowances (1cm). Cut a strip 3cm × 63/64cm for the buttonband.

Method

Make the shirt pattern, following the chart on pp. 36 and 37 and cut it out. Then cut out the fabric.

Attaching interfacing

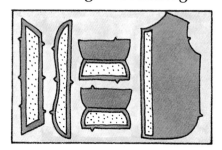

Iron interfacing on to wrong side of fabric with warm iron. Iron buttonband strip 5mm from edge on wrong side of right*front.

* Left front for boy's shirt.

Pleats

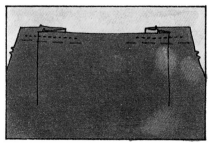

On back of shirt fold 2 pleats towards armholes, matching notches. Tack in place. Stitch across pleats close to top edge, to hold them in place.

What is a facing?

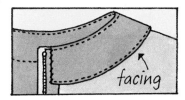

A facing is used to line and strengthen edges, such as necklines, armholes and yokes. It is usually made of the same fabric as the garment.

Trimming a seam allowance

Some seams are too bulky, even with a 1cm seam allowance (for example, on collars, yokes and curved seams). Carefully trim these seams to about 5mm.

Yoke

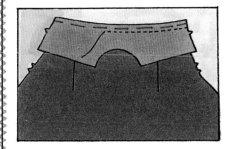

With right sides together and matching notches, pin shirt yoke to back and tack it in place. Stitch, making sure the pleats lie flat.

Pin right side of yoke facing to wrong side of back. Tack in place, then stitch along the seamline you made when stitching yoke to back.

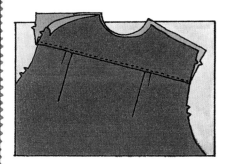

Trim seam allowance (see left) and fold yoke pieces upwards. Press together, as shown. Topstitch, just above the seamline.

Pocket

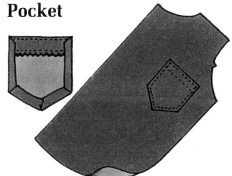

Neaten and turn in 3cm at top of pocket. Press. Stitch twice, as shown. Press 5mm turnings round rest of pocket and tack in place on shirt front. Topstitch.

Shoulder seams

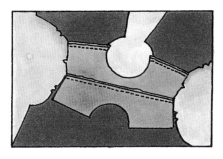

Match right side of yoke facing to wrong side of shirt front at shoulder seams. Tack. Stitch. Trim seams and press them towards yoke.

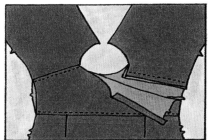

Lay shirt flat on table. Pin yoke pieces together. Turn under 1cm on yoke shoulders. Tack over raw edges, as shown. Topstitch close to folds.

Right front

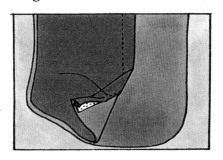

Turn in 5mm along long edge of right front*. Press. Stitch close to fold. Turn in another 3.5cm and press. Tack. Topstitch close to fold.

* Reverse instructions for the right and left fronts for a boy's shirt.

Left front

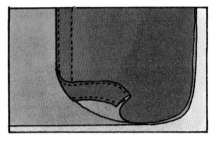

Turn in 4cm along left front. Tack. Press. Topstitch close to fold. Press 1cm to wrong side along raw edge. Stitch and press.

Sleeves

With right sides of fabric facing, pin sleeves into armholes, matching notches. Tack. Stitch, stretching fabric gently round curves.

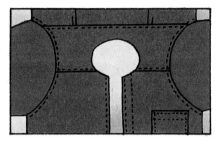

Neaten raw edges together with zig zag stitch. Press neatened edges towards body of shirt. Topstitch on body side of seamline.

Collar

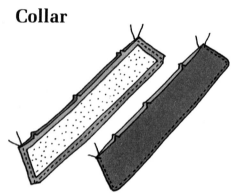

With right sides facing, tack collar pieces together round 3 sides. Stitch, clip corners and trim seam. Turn right way out. Topstitch as shown.

With right sides facing, tack edges of neckband to collar, as shown, matching notches. Stitch. Trim seam. Turn neckband right way out. Press.

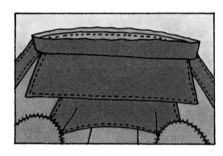

Tack inside edge of neckband to wrong side of neck edge of shirt, as shown, matching notches. Stitch neckband in place and trim seam allowance.

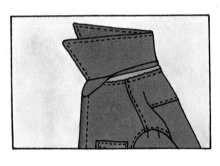

Press seam towards neckband. Press 1cm turning to wrong side along free edge of neckband. Turn it to right side of shirt.

Tack down free edge of neckband, so it covers raw edge on right side of shirt. Topstitch around side and bottom edges of neckband and press.

Side seams

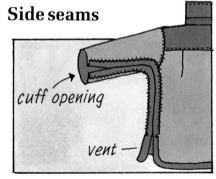

With right sides facing, tack sleeve and side seams, matching notches. Stitch from notch at sleeve opening to hem notch. Neaten raw edges apart.

Sleeve openings

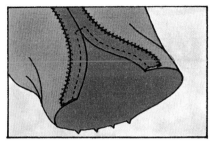

Tack down seam allowance at sleeve opening. Stitch around opening, about 5mm in, up one side, flat across top, and down other side.

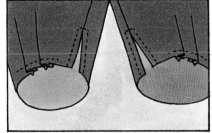

Matching notches, fold two pleats towards back of shirt on each sleeve. Tack down and stitch across tops of pleats to hold them in place.

Cuffs

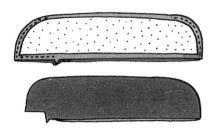

Fold cuffs as shown, right sides together. Tack round curved edge as far as notch. Stitch. Trim seam and clip corners. Turn right way out. Press.

Tack inside of cuff to sleeve, with right side of cuff facing wrong side of sleeve. Trim seam and press raw edge towards sleeve.

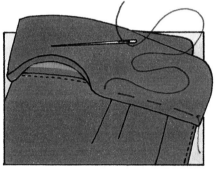

Turn in 1cm along free edge of cuff and press. Turn free edge of cuff over to right side of sleeve and tack it over raw edges of seam.

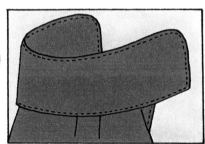

On the right side topstitch carefully all the way around each cuff, being careful not to pucker the fabric as you do so.

Hem

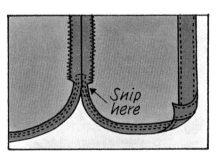

Turn in 5mm around bottom of shirt. Press and stitch. Turn in another 5mm to cover raw edges. Press and stitch as for sleeve openings.

Finishing

Make 6 buttonholes,* 1.25cm wide, down right** front, 7.5 mm from edge. Make top one in neckband, next one 3cm below and space the rest 10cm apart.

Make a buttonhole in each cuff, 1cm from left edge. Stitch buttons under buttonholes on left** front of shirt and halfway down each cuff overlap.

* See page 31 for machine stitched buttonholes
** Reverse instructions for the right and left fronts for a boy's shirt.

Baggy shirt pattern

Layout for fabric 115cm wide

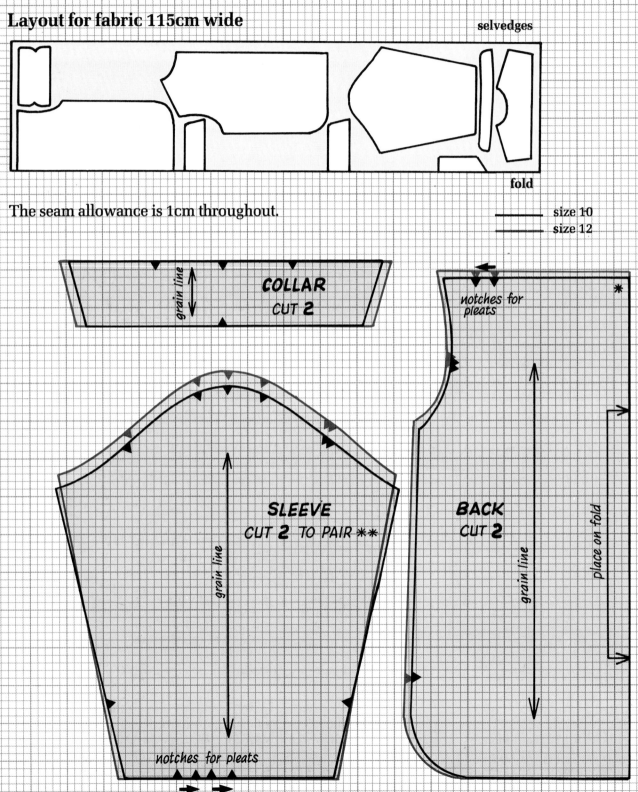

selvedges

fold

The seam allowance is 1cm throughout.

———	size 10
- - -	size 12

COLLAR
CUT **2**

grain line

notches for pleats

*

SLEEVE
CUT **2** TO PAIR **

grain line

notches for pleats

BACK
CUT **2**

grain line

place on fold

* If your fabric is 90cm wide, make a pattern piece for the complete back by cutting it on folded paper.

Layout for fabric 90cm wide

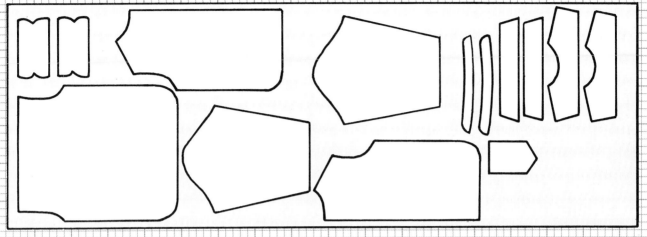

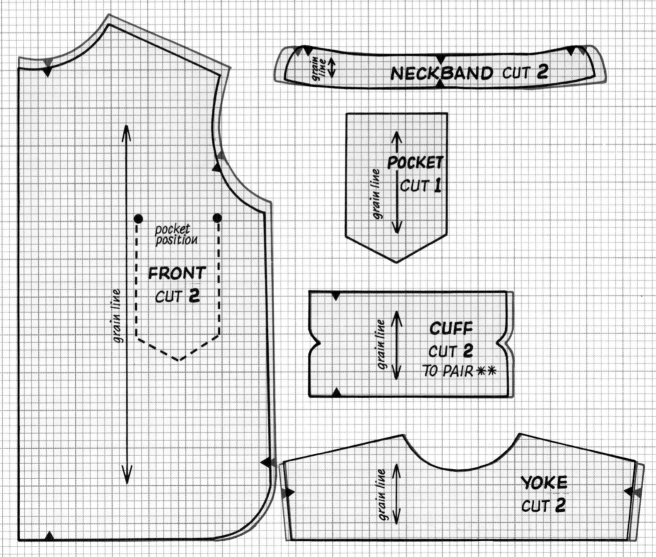

NECKBAND CUT **2**

POCKET CUT **1**

pocket position

FRONT CUT **2**

grain line

CUFF CUT **2** TO PAIR ******

YOKE CUT **2**

Jumpsuit

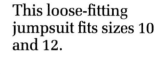

This loose-fitting jumpsuit fits sizes 10 and 12.

Sizes

To fit chest: 83/87cm
Finished size
Length: 147cm
Inside leg length: 73cm
Back body length: 80cm
Chest: 112cm
Underarm sleeve length: 43cm

Suggested fabrics

Fine cottons, seersucker, crinkle cotton, poplin, brushed cotton, Viyella

Method

Make the pattern, following the chart on pages 40 and 41 and cut out. Then cut out the fabric.

Centre back seam

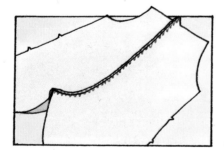

With right sides together, tack 2 back pieces together. Stitch, stretching fabric around the curve, neaten raw edges together and press to one side.

Centre front seam

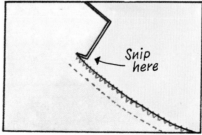

Snip here

Tack centre front seam, with right sides together. Stitch. Snip into corner at top of seam. Neaten raw edges together and press to one side.

Yoke

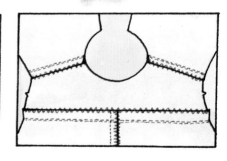

Stitch yoke to back, right sides together. Neaten raw edges together and press upwards. Topstitch. Stitch front shoulder and yoke seams in same way.

Pockets

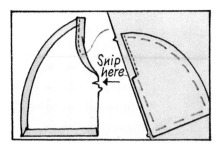

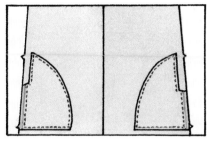

Turn in 1cm above notch on pocket edge. Press. Stitch 5mm in. Turn in 1cm along curved and bottom edges. Press. Tack to front, in line with notches.

Topstitch pockets round curves and bottom edges. Stitch raw edges of pockets to side edges of jumpsuit about 5mm in.

Sleeves and body seams

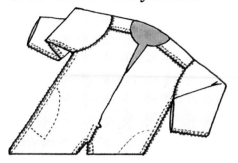

Sew in sleeves as for tee-shirt*. Tack underarm and side seams. Stitch. Neaten seams and press towards back. Stitch inside leg seams in the same way.

Facing

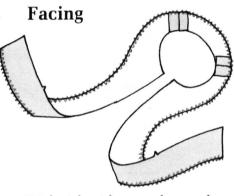

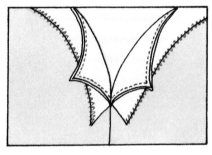

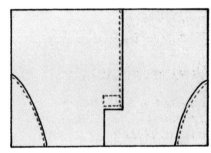

With right sides together, tack front facing to back neck facing at shoulder seams. Stitch. Press seams open. Zigzag round outside edge of facing.

Tack facing to neck and front openings so lower edge comes 1cm below front openings. Stitch round facing and across lower edge as far as centre front.

Trim seam, clip corners and turn right way out. Press. Topstitch, as shown. Lap right front over left at bottom of opening and topstitch a square.

Finishing

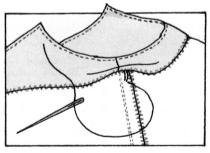

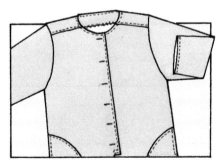

Lightly oversew facings to shoulder seams by hand**. Hem sleeves and legs, making first turning 5mm and second one 1cm. Topstitch.

Make 6 buttonholes♦ 1.5cm wide on right front, 7.5mm in from edge: top one 1.25cm below neck and five more spaced 10cm apart below that.

Stitch buttons under buttonholes on left front. Try on jumpsuit. Roll up sleeves and hems to right length. Oversew lightly at seams.

* See page 17   ** See page 42   ♦ See page 31 for machine stitched buttonholes

Jumpsuit pattern (one size)

Layout for fabric 90cm wide

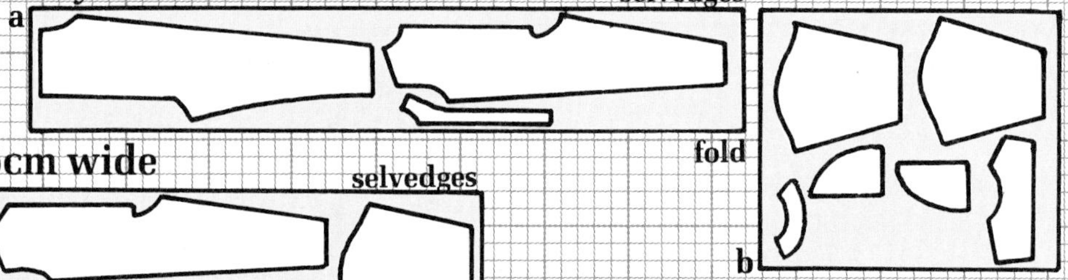

a

selvedges

fold

b

Layout for fabric 115cm wide

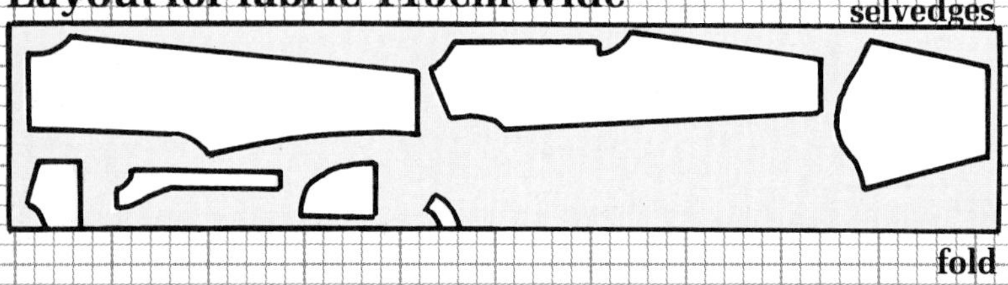

selvedges

fold

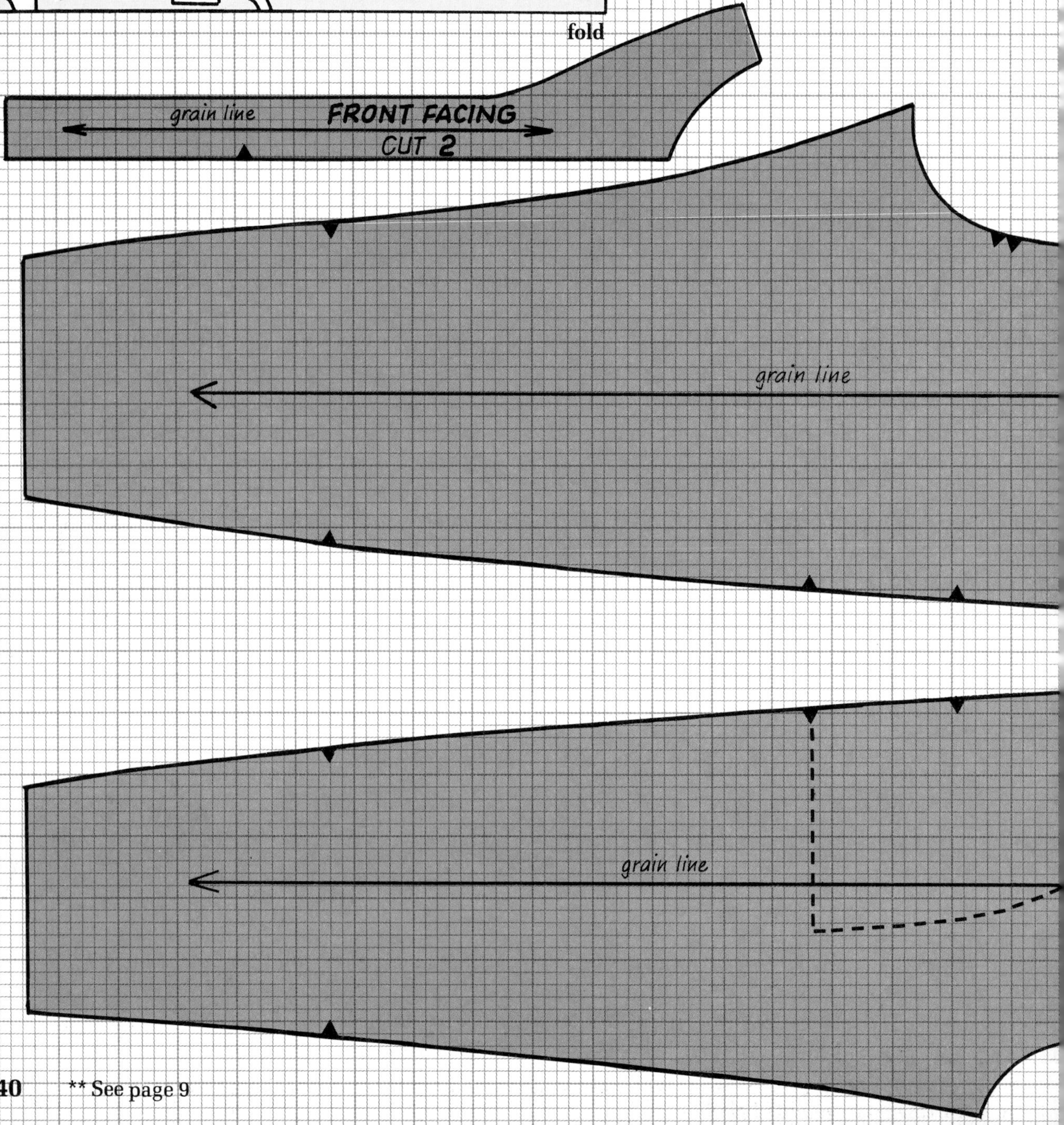

grain line **FRONT FACING**
CUT 2

grain line

grain line

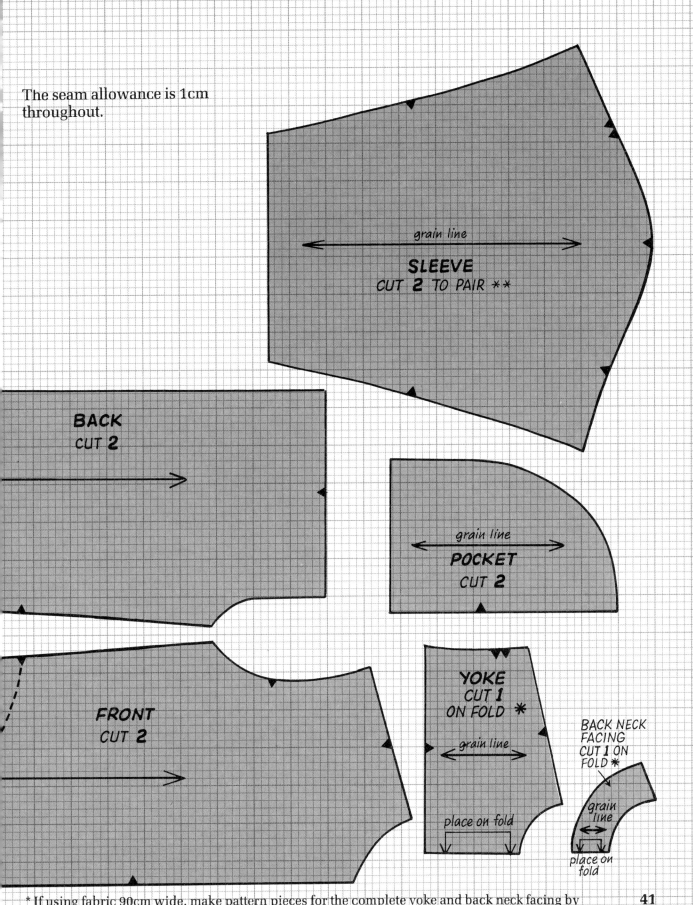

The seam allowance is 1cm throughout.

SLEEVE
CUT **2** TO PAIR ✱✱

grain line

BACK
CUT **2**

POCKET
CUT **2**

grain line

FRONT
CUT **2**

YOKE
CUT **1**
ON FOLD ✱

grain line

place on fold

BACK NECK
FACING
CUT **1** ON
FOLD ✱

grain
line

place on
fold

* If using fabric 90cm wide, make pattern pieces for the complete yoke and back neck facing by cutting them out on folded paper.   **41**

Basic hand sewing

Nearly everything you make needs some kind of hand sewing. It is used for tacking, neatening and finishing off clothes.

Here you can find out how to do some of the most useful stitches. Practise them on scraps of fabric before you start sewing.

Needles

The most useful general needles for hand sewing are called Sharps. Use fine needles for delicate fabrics and thicker ones for the heavier fabrics.

Thread

Use the same thread as you use for machining (see page 44). You can buy special thread for tacking.

Scissors

You will need a small pair of sharp scissors.

Things to remember

Start off your sewing on the wrong side of the fabric, by tying a knot in the end of the thread or by making a few tiny stitches on top of each other.

Try to make all the stitches the same size and do not pull the thread too tightly.

Tack everything before you hand sew it. Take the tacking out when you have finished and press your sewing.

Do not use too long a piece of thread for handsewing, or it will get knots in it.

Tacking

Tacking is big stitches. You tack things to hold them in position while you stitch them properly, then take the tacking out when you have finished.

For areas which need to be held more securely, such as curves, make the stitches smaller and sew them closer together.

Oversewing

If your machine does not have a zigzag stitch, oversew raw edges by hand to stop them from fraying.

Do not pull the thread too tightly or the edge of the fabric will pucker.

If the fabric is likely to fray badly, sew the stitches closer together.

Making a hem

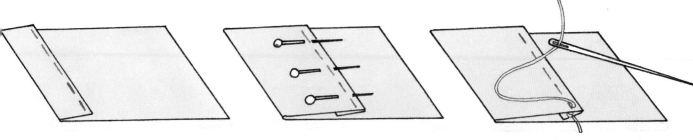

Turn the edge of the fabric in about 5mm. Tack it in place and press it.

Make a second turning the depth you want the hem. Pin and tack. Remove pins. Press.

Start with your knot or overstitching on the wrong side of the fabric.

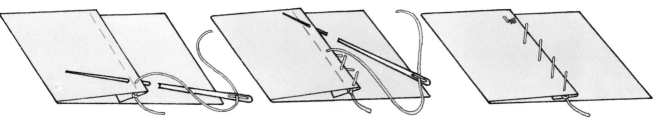

Catch two threads of the single layer of fabric and a stitch in the hem with the needle, as shown.

Carry on, keeping the stitches even. Do not pull the threads too tight.

When you reach the end, finish off with several small stitches on top of each other.

Making a buttonhole

Draw a pencil rectangle on the fabric the width you want the buttonhole to be. Draw a line half-way across and slit it.

Work from right to left. Secure the thread with backstitch on the wrong side and bring the needle through to the right side.

Put the needle through the slit and bring it up on the pencil line. Loop the thread round it. Pull it through to make a knot.

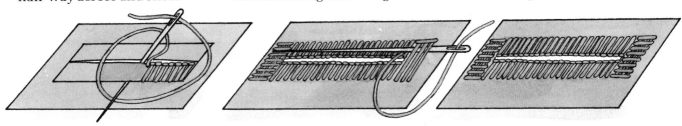

Start the second stitch close to the first one. Continue until you reach the end of the buttonhole.

Make 3 stitches the width of the whole buttonhole, as shown, then work the smaller stitches crosswise over the top.

Stitch the other side of the buttonhole. Neaten the end as before. Finish off with backstitch on the wrong side.

43

Choosing fabric and thread

There is a vast choice of different fabrics. You can buy them from department stores or fabric shops. Market stalls are good places to look too, but make sure you know what kind of fabric you are buying.

If you are just beginning to make clothes, choose firm, light to medium weight fabrics to start with as they are easiest to sew. Here you can find out about the main types of fabric.

Natural fabrics

Cotton

Light to medium weight. Different types, such as poplin (thick and crisp), lawn (fine) and voile (very fine). Easy to sew, but creases.

Wool

Warm and does not crease much. Use fine wool to make dresses, medium weight wool to make skirts and the heavier wools to make coats and jackets.

Corduroy

Thick, ribbed and has a 'pile' (see 'What is a nap?').

Viyella

Wool and cotton mixture. Warm. Good for shirts and dresses.

Jersey

Stretchy. Can be made of cotton or wool. Cotton jersey is good for sweatshirts and sportswear. Wool jersey is expensive and is used mainly for winter dresses.

Silk

Fine and expensive. Can be hard to sew because it is slippery. Used for party clothes.

Linen

Medium-weight, comfortable to wear. Expensive and creases easily. Used for summer clothes.

Threads

Choose thread to match the fabric you are sewing. Use cotton thread with natural fabrics, silk thread with silk and synthetic thread with man-made fabrics and jersey.

Buy thread a shade darker than your fabric as it looks lighter when you sew it.

You can buy special fine thread for tacking.

What are synthetics?

Synthetics are man-made fibres such as polyester, acrylic and nylon. They are cheaper than natural fabrics. You can buy mixtures of synthetic and natural fabrics which are easy to sew and wash.

Things you should know

Most fabrics are either knitted or woven. Knitted fabric, or jersey, is stretchy; woven fabric is firmer. The threads that run down it are called warp threads. Those that run from side to side are called weft threads. If you pull the fabric diagonally, you will find the 'bias'. This is the direction with most stretch.

The smooth, warp edges of woven fabrics are called selvedges.

What is a nap?

Some fabric has a 'pile' or furry surface, which feels smooth if you stroke it one way, but rough if you stroke it the other way. This is called a 'nap'. See page 9 to find out how to cut out napped fabric.

Fabrics such as taffeta which reflect the light in different ways also have a nap.

Patterned fabric

Some patterns are woven or knitted into the fabric, others are printed on. If a pattern is printed, the fabric has a right and wrong side. The pattern is fainter on the wrong side.

If your pattern goes in only one direction, treat it as though it has a nap (see above).

Things to remember

Take your pattern with you when buying fabric. Fabric comes in different widths and the pattern tells you how much of a width you need. It also suggests suitable fabrics for the garments you are making.

Make sure you choose the right type and weight of fabric for the time of year.

Look for fabrics which are easy to sew and washable. Scrunch a fabric in your hand to see if it creases easily.

Colour

Check that the colour suits you. Stand in front of a mirror and hold the fabric up to your face.

If the colour has to match other clothes, take them to the shop with you.

Artificial light can change the colour of a fabric. Ask the shop assistant if you can take it to a doorway or window to look at it in daylight.

Taking your measurements

To make your own clothes, you need to know your measurements. Patterns come in numbered, standard sizes, which are based on standard chest, waist and hip measurements.

All patterns allow some 'ease', so that the garments you make allow room for movement. You do not need to buy a size larger than you really take.

Before you start

Measure yourself in your underwear to get your accurate measurements.

You might find it helpful to ask a friend to take some of the measurements.

How to measure your chest, waist and hips

Measure your chest around the fullest part.

You can find your natural waistline by holding the tape measure loosely around your waist area and wriggling about a bit.

Measure your hips around the widest part when you are standing with your legs together.

Jot your measurements down and take them to the shop with you when you buy the pattern.

Other useful measurements

Your back length measurement is the distance between the bone at the base of your neck and your waist.

To find your sleeve length, bend your arm and measure from the top of your shoulder, over the curve of your elbow to your wrist.

You need to know your inside leg measurement when making trousers. Measure from your crotch to your ankle.

Finding your size

Look up your chest measurement on the chart. The waist and hip measurements should be about the same as yours too. Find out your size at the top of the chart.

	Metric Sizes				Imperial Sizes			
	8	10	12	14	8	10	12	14
Chest	80cm	83cm	87cm	92cm	31½"	32½"	34"	36"
Waist	61cm	64cm	67cm	71cm	24"	25"	26½"	28"
Hips	85cm	88cm	92cm	97cm	33½"	34½"	36"	38"

Understanding patterns

A pattern gives you a lot of information. Here are the main things you need to know.

The front of the pattern

If you have not made any clothes before, choose a simple pattern to start with and make sure you buy it for your size.

The back of the pattern

This gives you a brief description of the design.

View

A pattern sometimes gives you 2 or 3 versions of the same basic style. Check how much fabric you need for your version.

Suggested fabrics

It is best to choose one of the recommended fabrics.

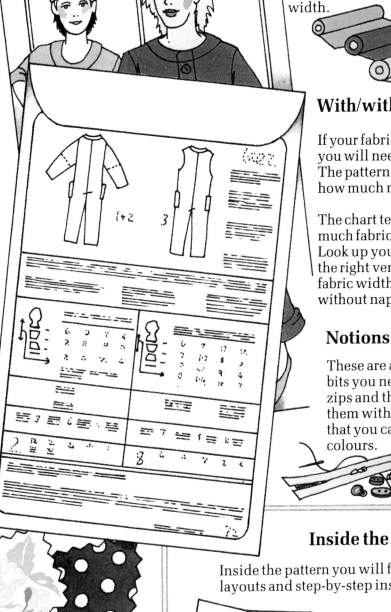

Fabric width

Fabric is made in three standard widths: 90cm, 115cm and 150cm. The pattern tells you how much fabric you would need to buy in each width.

With/without nap

If your fabric has a nap, you will need more of it. The pattern tells you how much more.

The chart tells you how much fabric you need. Look up your size and the right version, the fabric width and with/without nap.

Notions

These are all the extra bits you need, such as zips and thread. Buy them with the fabric so that you can match the colours.

Inside the pattern

Inside the pattern you will find fabric layouts and step-by-step instructions.

Restrictions

This tells you which fabrics to avoid using.

Lengthening or shortening patterns

Shop patterns usually give you a lengthening/shortening line so you can alter the length to fit you if you are taller or shorter than average for your size.

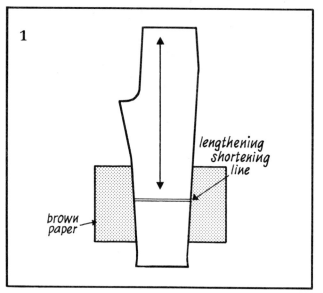

To lengthen the pattern, lay the lengthening/shortening line on a piece of brown paper or squared pattern paper which is big enough to allow for the extra length you want and at least the same width as the pattern itself.

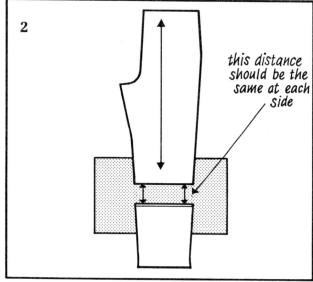

Cut along the line and move the lower half of the pattern down until you have the extra length you want between the two pieces of the pattern. Measure the gap in between at each side to make sure the pattern is straight.

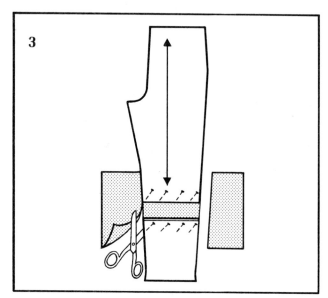

Pin or tape both pieces of the pattern on to the brown paper along the cut lines. Join up the pattern outline using a pencil and a ruler. Trim off the spare brown paper or squared paper with a pair of scissors.

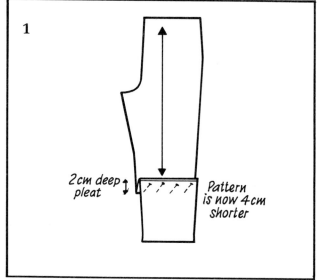

To shorten a pattern, make a pleat in it at the lengthening/shortening line. Make it half the depth of the amount you want to take out. For example if you want to shorten the pattern by 4cm, make the pleat 2cm deep. Pin in place.

PART TWO
KNITTING

Angela Wilkes and Carol Garbera

Illustrated by Lily Whitlock

Designed by Roger Priddy

CONTENTS

50　About knitting

52　Yarns

54　Things you need

56　Starting to knit

58　The basic stitches

60　Following a pattern

61　Knitting things the right size

62　Anklewarmers and mittens

64　Scarf with pockets

66　Bobble hat

68　Cotton vest

70　Tube skirt

72　Pink sweater

76　Striped sweaters

77　Baggy square sweater

78　Picture knitting

80　Blue jacket

84　Aran sweater

89　Making your knitting fit

90　Increasing and decreasing

92　Finishing your knitting

94　Putting mistakes right

96　Index

Additional illustrations by John Shackell, Roger Priddy and Christine Berrington.

About knitting

Many people know how to knit but have never tried to knit themselves a sweater. This book shows you that knitting is a lot easier than you might think. It gives you patterns for things you will want both to make and wear and shows you what to do as you go along. The patterns start with easy things and progress in difficulty so that by the end of the book you can tackle an Aran sweater.

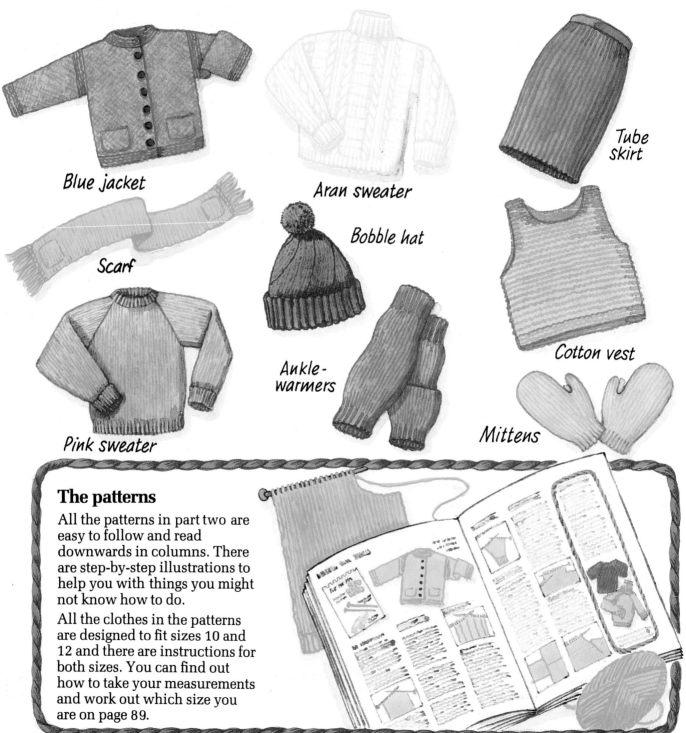

Blue jacket

Scarf

Aran sweater

Bobble hat

Ankle-warmers

Pink sweater

Tube skirt

Cotton vest

Mittens

The patterns

All the patterns in part two are easy to follow and read downwards in columns. There are step-by-step illustrations to help you with things you might not know how to do.

All the clothes in the patterns are designed to fit sizes 10 and 12 and there are instructions for both sizes. You can find out how to take your measurements and work out which size you are on page 89.

Knitting Know How

From this book you can learn the basics of how to knit and also how to do the more fancy stitches, how to knit cables and do circular knitting.

Techniques

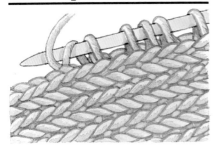

You can learn all the basic knitting techniques and skills, such as how to pick up stitches round a neck, or finish off your knitting.

Things you need

On the next few pages you can find out all about the different types of yarn you can buy, knitting needles and other useful things to have.

Following a pattern

*K2 tog, P2tog, repeat from * to end of row

Many knitting patterns you buy seem hard to understand at first. On page 60 you can find out how to follow a pattern and what the abbreviations mean.

Making mistakes

Every knitter drops a stitch or makes a mistake from time to time. Don't panic. On page 94 you can find out how to put your mistakes right.

Variations

The first part of each pattern shows you, step-by-step, how to make a basic garment, and at the end of the pattern there are suggestions on how to adapt it. You can find out how to make it longer or shorter, how to alter the basic shape, how to knit it in stripes or knit a number or letter on it. These variations also show you how you can try out and experiment with your own design ideas.

Yarns

There is an enormous choice of yarns available. Some are made from natural fibres, such as wool or cotton, and others from synthetic fibres. Many of the more exotic yarns are made from mixtures of different fibres. Here you can find out about the main types of yarn and what you need to know when buying them.

Natural fibres

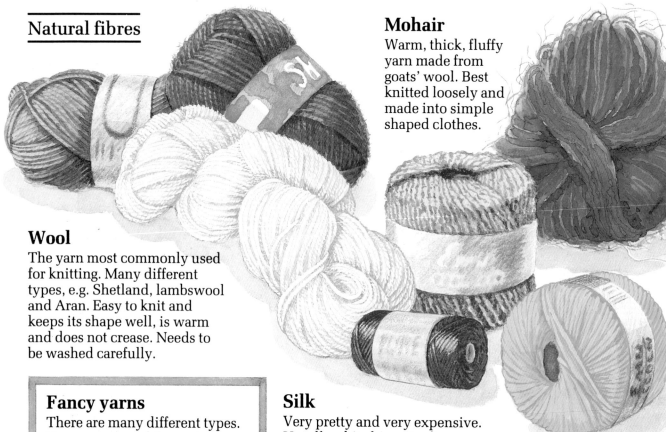

Mohair
Warm, thick, fluffy yarn made from goats' wool. Best knitted loosely and made into simple shaped clothes.

Wool
The yarn most commonly used for knitting. Many different types, e.g. Shetland, lambswool and Aran. Easy to knit and keeps its shape well, is warm and does not crease. Needs to be washed carefully.

Fancy yarns
There are many different types. Here are some of the main ones.

slubs

chenille

glitter yarns

bouclé

ribbon / tape

Silk
Very pretty and very expensive. Usually a bit shiny. Is often mixed with wool or cotton to make it cheaper.

Synthetic yarns
These include acrylics, polyesters, nylon and viscose. Strong, light and easy to wash. Not as warm as wool. Often mixed with natural fibres to make stronger, cheaper yarns.

Cotton
Good for summer sweaters. Many types available – plain, fancy, shiny and matt. Sometimes mixed with linen. Hardwearing and easy to wash.

How thick are different yarns?

—————— *fine* —————— *average* —————— *thick* —————— *very thick* —

2 ply   **3 ply**   **4 ply**   **Double knitting**   **Aran**   **Chunky**   **Icelandic**

Yarns are made of spun fibres, called plys, which are twisted together. A 3 ply yarn, for example, contains three strands of fibre. The number of plys does not necessarily tell you how thick the yarn is as the plys can be thick or thin, depending on the types of yarn. This is a rough guide to which types of yarn are fine and which ones are thick.

About your yarn

Knitting patterns always tell you how much yarn you need. Yarn is sold by weight. Every ball of yarn has a paper label which tells you how much it weighs and gives you other useful information.

The yarn label tells you what the yarn is made of and where it was made.

It also gives you washing instructions for the yarn. Always keep a label for future reference.

This symbol shows you what size needles to use.

This number refers to the colour of the yarn. If you want to know which colours are available in a particular yarn, ask the shop assistant to show you the shade chart.

Yarn is dyed in batches or 'lots' and always has a lot number. Every time a new lot is dyed, the dye is made again, so it varies a little from one lot to another. Make sure that all the yarn you buy for any one garment has the same lot number.

Things you need

All you need to start knitting is a pair of needles and some yarn, but there are different types of needles for different types of knitting. Below you can find out what they are.

There are also some gadgets which can help to make knitting easier. You can read about them on the opposite page.

Single-pointed needles

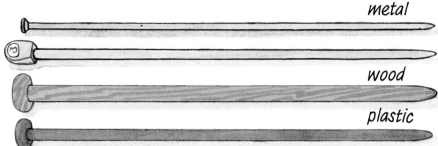

metal

wood

plastic

These are the needles you usually knit with. They are sized according to how thick they are. The thicker the needle, the bigger the stitches it makes. You can buy long or short knitting needles. The shorter ones are usually easier to use unless you are knitting something with a lot of stitches.

Cable needle

You use this to hold a group of stitches when you are knitting cables. It should be the same size or smaller than the other needles you are using.

Double pointed needles

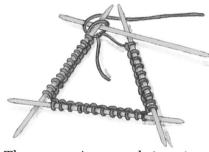

These come in normal sizes, in sets of six or four. You use them to knit small, tubular things without a seam, such as polo necks or socks.

Circular needle

You use a circular needle to knit seamless, tubular things, such as skirts. You can buy them in different lengths, so check what your pattern says.

Needle sizes

Nowadays you buy needles in metric sizes, but many people still have needles in English sizes. In this chart you can see which sizes correspond to which.

Continental (mm)	2¼	2¾	3	3¼	3¾	4	4½	5	5½	6	6½	7	7½	8½	9
English	13	12	11	10	9	8	7	6	5	4	3	2	1	00	000
U.S.	0	1	2	3	4	5	6	7	8	9	10	10½	11	13	15

Other useful things

Stitch holder

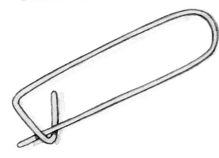

Like a giant safety pin. On it you keep stitches which you are not knitting, until you are ready to knit them. It is a good idea to have at least two.

Row counter

This helps you to keep track of how many rows you have knitted. You slip it on to the end of a needle and turn it as you finish each row.

Needle guards

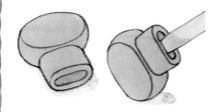

You put these on the points of your needles when you are not knitting so that you do not drop stitches. They also help protect your knitting bag.

Tapestry or darning needles

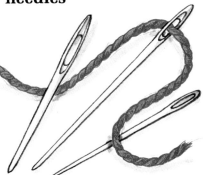

Large, blunt-ended needles like these are best for sewing up your pieces of knitting.

Long pins

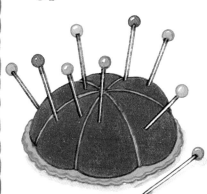

For pinning your knitting out before pressing it or sewing it together.

Small sharp scissors

For cutting yarn and trimming loose yarn ends.

Tape measure

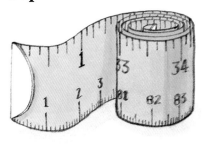

To check your tension is right (see page 61) and to measure your knitting.

Crochet hook

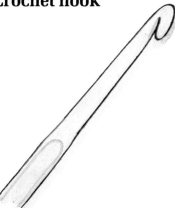

For picking up dropped stitches.

Knitting gauge

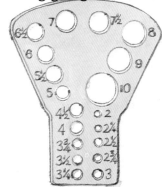

You can use this to check the metric sizes of your knitting needles and crochet hooks.

Starting to knit

Making the first row of stitches on a needle is called casting on. There are many ways to cast on, but the way shown here is easy and gives knitting a firm edge.

The two main knitting stitches are called knit and purl. If you have not knitted before, find a pair of needles and some leftover yarn. Cast on 20 stitches and practise doing knit and purl before you try to knit anything.

Casting on

Wind the yarn round your finger and pull a loop through it. Slip it on to a knitting needle and pull it to make a stitch.

Hold this needle in your left hand. Put your right needle into the stitch and wind the yarn under and around it.

How to knit

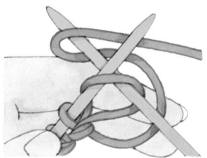

With the yarn at the back, slip the right needle into the first stitch on the left needle. Wind the yarn around it as shown.

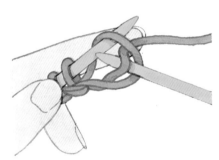

Pull the loop of yarn towards you through the stitch on the left needle.

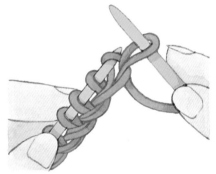

Push the right needle forwards and slide the old stitch off the left needle, keeping the new stitch on the right needle.

How to purl

With the yarn at the front, put the right needle into the front of the first stitch on the left needle, from right to left.

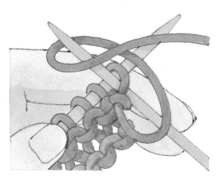

Wind the yarn over and around the point of the right needle anticlockwise, as shown.

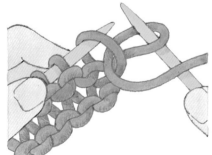

Pull the loop of yarn backwards through the stitch on the left needle and push the old stitch towards the tip of the needle.

56

Then pull a loop through with the point of the right needle to make a stitch and slip it on to the left needle.

To make the next stitch, put the right needle between the two stitches, wind the yarn around it and carry on as before.

Make the rest of the stitches in the same way. Start each one by putting the needle between the two last stitches.

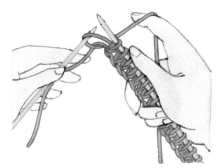

Carry on to the end of the row. To start a new row, turn the knitting round and hold the full needle in your left hand.

Slide the old stitch off the end of the left needle, keeping the new stitch on the right needle. Carry on like this along the row.

How to hold the needles and yarn

If you thread the yarn between your fingers when knitting, it helps you to knit faster and more evenly.

Holding the yarn in your right hand

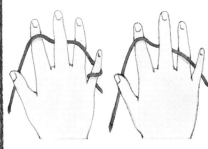

You use your right forefinger to wind the yarn round the needles.

Holding the yarn in your left hand

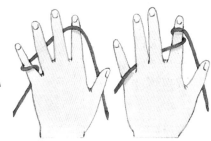

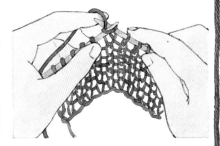

You use your left forefinger to wind the yarn round the needles.

The basic stitches

All knitting stitches are made up of knit and purl used in different combinations. Here are the main stitches you need to know. They are used in most of the patterns in this book.

To practise them, use odd scraps of double knitting yarn and size 4mm needles. Cast on 20 stitches and knit 20 rows, then cast off. You can see how to do this at the bottom of the page.

Garter stitch

The easiest stitch to do. Just knit every stitch of every row. (You can also do it by purling every stitch of every row).

Stocking stitch

Knit one row, then purl one row throughout. Looks like jersey on the right side and fine garter stitch on the wrong side.

Ribbing 1

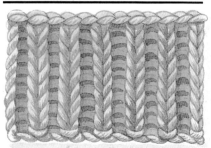

Knit 1, bring yarn forwards, purl 1, take yarn back. Repeat these 2 stitches to end of row. On the next row, knit the purl stitches and purl the knit ones.

Ribbing 2

Knit 2, bring yarn forwards, purl 2, take yarn back. Repeat these 4 stitches to end of row. On the next row, knit the purl stitches and purl the knit ones.

Moss stitch

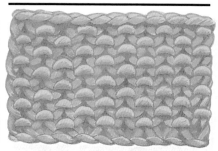

Knit one, bring yarn forwards, purl one, take yarn back. Repeat to end of row. On the next row, knit the knit stitches and purl the purl stitches.

How to cast off

When you have finished your knitting, you "cast off". This means that you knit the stitches off the needle to make a neat edge which does not come undone.

It is best to cast off on a knit row, but if you do cast off on a purl row, purl all of the stitches instead of knitting them. When casting off ribbing, keep to the rib pattern and use both knit and purl. Always cast off loosely.

Knit the first two stitches in the row. With the yarn at the back of the work, put the left needle into the first stitch.

Lift the first stitch over the second one, as shown, and drop it off the needle so that only the second stitch is left.

Knitting Hints

These hints should help you if you are just starting to knit.

Try to knit evenly. The stitches should be just loose enough for you to put a needle into them easily.

If you are a beginner knitter, count your stitches at the end of every row, to check that you have not dropped one.

Do not worry if you have dropped a stitch or made a mistake. You can find out how to put mistakes right on p. 94

Always finish the row you are knitting. If you stop in the middle of a row, you will get an uneven stitch and you could easily drop a stitch.

Knitting quickly comes with practise, so always try to knit a few rows at a time. If you want to knit something quick, choose something small that you knit on big needles.

Keep your knitting and all your knitting things together in a bag so that you do not lose anything. It will also help to keep your knitting clean.

Knit another stitch, then lift the first stitch over the second one as before. Carry on like this along the row.

When you reach the last stitch, break off the yarn, slip it through the stitch and pull it, to tighten the loop.

When you finish off your knitting, thread the end of yarn on to a darning needle and darn it into the edge of the knitting.

Following a pattern

Knitting patterns often seem difficult to read. The patterns in part 2 have been clearly laid out under different headings so that they are easy to follow. Here you can find out what each part of the pattern tells you. In the column on the right you will find a list of the abbreviations most commonly used in knitting patterns.

You will need:
1 ball double knitting
size 7mm needles
stitch holder

This tells you which type of yarn and what size needles to use. It also tells you if there is anything else you need – such as stitch holders or buttons.

Tension

This tells you how many stitches and rows you should have to each centimeter you knit. You can find out more about this on the opposite page.

Measurements

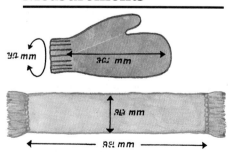

The diagram shows you what the measurements of the finished garment should be.

Sizes

In patterns for two sizes, the smaller size, or the figures that apply to it, are printed first, and the larger size comes after it in brackets.

Big   Small

Where there is just one figure, it applies to both sizes. If you underline the figures that apply to your size before you start, you will be able to pick them out more easily as you knit.

Method

The knitting instructions are written in columns. Whenever you stop knitting, make a pencil mark on the pattern, so you do not lose your place.

Making up

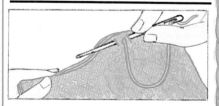

This tells you how to finish off what you are making and how to sew it up. You can find out more about this on pages 92/93.

Abbreviations

This list covers all the most common knitting abbreviations. You can find out more about the terms used on the page numbers shown.

beg	beginning
cm	centimetre
cont	continue
dec	decrease (p.91)
garter st	garter stitch (p.58)
inc	increase (p.90)
k	knit
k2tog	knit 2 stitches together (p.91)
kwise	knitwise (insert needle as if to knit)
m1	make 1 (p.91)
p	purl
psso	pass slip stitch over
pwise	purlwise (insert needle as if to purl)
rem	remaining
rep	repeat
sl	slip a stitch to the other needle without knitting it.
sl st	slip stitch
tbl	through back of loop
tog	together
yrn	yarn round needle

Asterisks

Asterisks mark a pattern section that has to be repeated. "Repeat from * to end" means you have to keep repeating the pattern section to the end of the row.

Knitting things the right size

If you want the things you knit to finish up the right size, your knitting must be the right tightness or "tension". If you knit too tightly, your knitting will end up too small.

If you knit too loosely, your garment will end up too big.

The type of yarn, size of needle and stitch you use all affect the size of your knitting.

Every knitting pattern gives you the tension for that pattern. Always check your tension using the recommended yarn before you start knitting. It does not take long and can save a lot of disappointment later.

How to check your tension

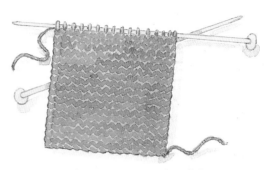

Knit a sample square, using the right yarn, needles and stitch. It is best to make it a little bigger than the tension given in the pattern. For example, if the pattern says 22 sts and 32 rows = 10 cm, cast on 26 stitches and knit 36 rows, then cast off.

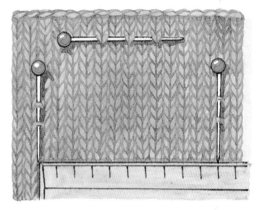

Smooth the square out on a flat surface without stretching it, then mark out a 10 cm square with pins. Lay a tape measure across the knitting and count every stitch and half stitch between the pins. Count the rows in the same way.

Too loose or too tight?

If there are too many stitches and rows in the pinned area, your knitting is too tight. Knit another sample with needles a size larger. If there are too few stitches and rows, your knitting is too loose. Knit a square with needles a size smaller.

Ankle warmers

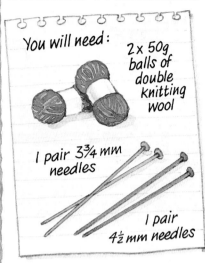

You will need:
2 x 50g balls of double knitting wool

1 pair 3¾ mm needles

1 pair 4½ mm needles

Tension

20 sts and 29 rows – 10cm in st st using size 4½mm needles.

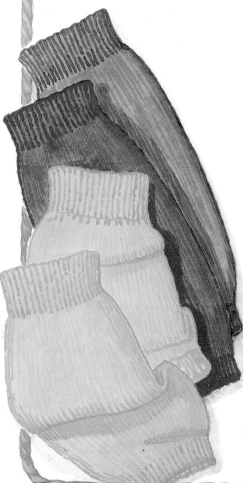

Method

With size 3¾mm needles cast on 58 sts and knit 4cm in k1,p1 rib.

Change to 4½mm needles. Cont in stocking stitch until work measures 28cm from beginning.

Change back to 3¾mm needles and knit 6cm in k1,p1 rib. Cast off loosely. Knit the 2nd anklewarmer in the same way.

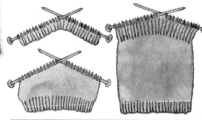

Making up

Lightly press wrong side of stocking stitch*. Fold anklewarmers in half lengthways, right sides together. Sew up side seams, using a flat seam.

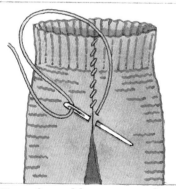

Turn the anklewarmers the right way out. Wear them with the longer ribbing at the top.

Measurements

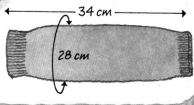

34 cm

28 cm

Mittens

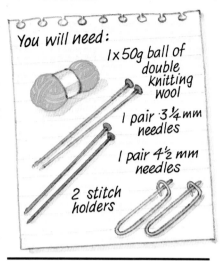

You will need:
1 x 50g ball of double knitting wool

1 pair 3¼ mm needles

1 pair 4½ mm needles

2 stitch holders

Tension

As for anklewarmers

Method

With size 3¼mm needles cast on 40 sts and work in k2,p2 rib for 6cm.

Change to 4½mm needles. Starting with a knit row, work 2 rows st st.

Next row K19, k twice into next st, k twice into next st, k19 – 42 sts.

Work 3 rows in st st, starting with a purl row.

Next row K19, k twice into next st, k2, k twice into next st, k19 – 44 sts.

Starting with a purl row, cont straight in st st for 7 rows. Break off wool.

Thumb

Slip the first 16 sts on to a stitch holder.

Rejoin wool and knit next 12 sts.

Slip the last 16 sts on to a stitch holder.

Next row Purl twice into first st, p11, p twice into last st – 14sts.

Starting with a k row, work straight in st st for 14 rows.

* See p.92

Shape top of thumb

1st row K2tog along row – 7sts.
2nd row P2tog 3 times, p1–7sts.
Break wool, thread it through
rem sts with a darning needle
and sew it firmly.

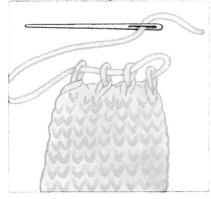

Hand

Rejoin wool to right side. Knit
16 sts on 1st stitch holder, pick
up 1st st from each side of base
of thumb, k16 sts on 2nd holder
– 34sts. Cont in st st until work
measures 21.5cm from beg.

Shape top of hand

1st row K2tog, k13, k2tog,
k2tog, k13, k2tog – 30 sts.
2nd, 4th, 6th row Purl
3rd row K2tog, k11, k2tog,
k2tog, k11, k2tog – 26sts.
5th row K2tog, k9, k2tog, k2tog,
k9, k2tog.
7th row Cast off.

Making up

Lightly press stocking stitch on
wrong side. Fold mittens in
half, right sides together. Sew
up thumbs with flat seams,
using the thread left at the top
of it. Sew up outside seams of
mitten, using a flat seam. Turn
mittens right way out and press.

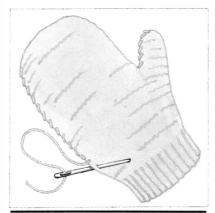

Measurements

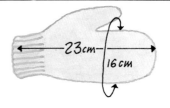

Scarf with pockets

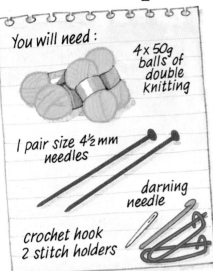

You will need:

4 x 50g balls of double knitting

1 pair size 4½mm needles

darning needle

crochet hook
2 stitch holders

This scarf is knitted in easy garter stitch. You can knit it in a plain colour with pockets or make it striped.

Tension

20sts and 32 rows = 10cm in garter stitch, using size 4½mm needles.

Length excluding tassels — 112cm

Width: 22.5 cm

Pocket

With size 4½mm needles cast on 22 sts and knit 11cm of garter st. Leave the sts on a stitch holder.

Main piece

Cast on 48 sts and work in garter st for 12cm. If you slip the 1st stitch in every row without knitting it, it will give the scarf firm edges.

Joining yarn

When you finish a ball of yarn, join the new one at the beginning of a row. Start the row with the new yarn, holding the two ends of yarn together. Knit the row, then tie the ends together. Sew them in later.

Adding the pocket

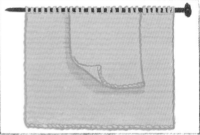

Next row K13, cast off next 22 sts, k to end of row.
Next row K13, knit across the 22 sts at the top of the pocket, k to end of row.
Continue straight until work measures 99cm from beginning.

Second pocket

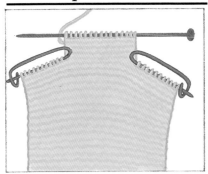

Knit 13 sts and put them on a holder, k22, put the last 13 sts on to a holder. Cont straight on rem 22 sts for 11cm. Cast off.

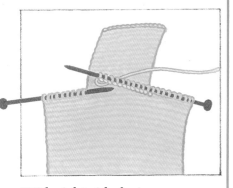

With right side facing you, rejoin wool. Slip the first 13 sts back on to needle. Cast on 22 sts, then knit 2nd group of 13 sts (48 sts altogether). Cont straight for 12cm. Cast off.

Making Up

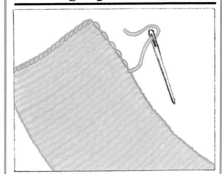

Neatly sew the loose ends of wool into the sides of the scarf and sew them firmly in place with small stitches.

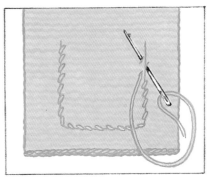

Sew the two pockets in place. Lay them flat against the wrong side of the scarf, then carefully oversew the three free sides. Sew the ends of yarn firmly in place with small stitches.

Making the tassels

Wind wool around a small book, then cut down one side to make lengths of wool. You need 180 lengths about 20cm long. Divide them into groups of 10.

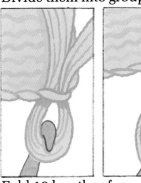

Fold 10 lengths of wool in half and pull them through the bottom edge of the scarf, from front to back, with a crochet hook. Pull the ends firmly through the loop to make a knotted tassel.

Make 9 tassels at each end of the scarf and trim the ends.

Striped scarf

To knit a scarf in two colours you need 2 x 50g balls of each colour.

Fine stripes

Leave out the pockets and work alternate stripes two rows deep. When knitting the stripes, carry the colour not being used loosely up the side of the work until it is needed. Make the tassels in alternate colours.

Wide stripes

Knit each stripe 10cm deep. Join the colour for each new stripe as you would a new ball of wool.

Bobble hat

You will need:
3 x 50g balls double knitting wool

1 pair 3¼ mm needles
1 pair 4½ mm needles

piece of card 8cm x 16cm

scissors
darning needle

Measurements

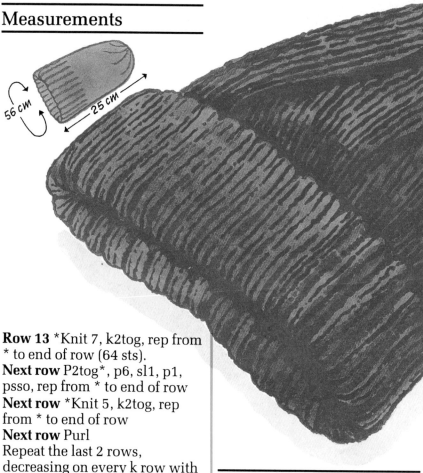

56 cm

25 cm

Tension

20 sts and 29 rows = 10cm in stocking stitch, using size 4½mm needles.

Method

With 3¼mm needles cast on 120 sts and work in k2,p2 rib for 11cm. Change to 4½mm needles and cont in st st, starting with a k row, until hat measures 16cm from beginning.

Shaping

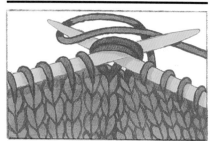

Row 1 *K13, k2tog, rep from * to end of row (112 sts).
Row 2 and every alternate row Purl
Row 3 *Knit 12, k2tog, rep from * to end of row (104 sts).
Carry on decreasing on every knit row, with one less st between decreases each time until you have knitted 12 rows from beg of shaping (72 sts).

Row 13 *Knit 7, k2tog, rep from * to end of row (64 sts).
Next row P2tog*, p6, sl1, p1, psso, rep from * to end of row
Next row *Knit 5, k2tog, rep from * to end of row
Next row Purl
Repeat the last 2 rows, decreasing on every k row with one less st between the decreases each row until there are 16 sts left, ending with a purl row.

Top of the hat

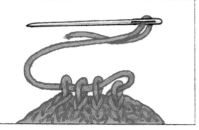

Next row K2tog all along row (8sts).
Next row P2tog all along row (4sts).
Break wool and thread it through the last 4 sts with a darning needle.

Making Up

Lay the hat over the end of an ironing board and lightly press the st st area on the wrong side.

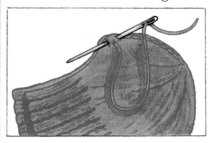

Fold the hat in half, right sides together. Sew the wool left at the top of the hat firmly in place, then backstitch the side seam as far as the ribbing. Turn the hat right side out and sew up the ribbing with a flat seam.

Making the bobble

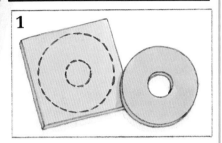

1

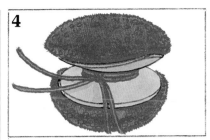

Draw 2 circles 7cm in diameter on card. In the centre of each circle draw a circle 2cm across. Cut them out to make two rings.

2

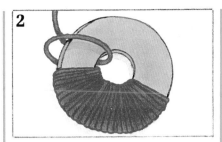

Put the two card rings together and wind wool evenly round them. Use a darning needle to do this when the hole is small.

3

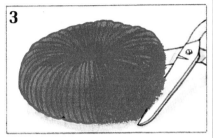

When the hole is full, cut round the edges of the circles through all the layers of wool between the card rings.

4

Ease the card rings apart and tie a double length of wool tightly round the middle of the bobble. Leave the long ends free.

5

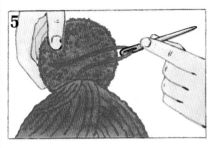

Remove the card rings and fluff out the bobble. Use the long ends of wool to sew the bobble on top of the hat.

How to knit stripes

You can make a striped hat, mittens or anklewarmers. Here are the amounts of yarn you will need and some ideas for different types of narrow stripes.

Mittens

2 × 50g balls double knitting wool in contrasting colours.

Work 2 rows st st in each colour in turn. Carry the colour not being used up the side of the work until needed.

Hat

2 × 50g balls main colour
1 × 50g ball contrast colour

Work 4 rows st st in one colour, then 2 rows in the other. Repeat to end. Make the bobble out of both colours.

Anklewarmers

2 × 50g balls main colour
1 × 50g ball contrast colour

Work 4 rows st st in each colour in turn. Backstitch the seams so the loops do not show on right side of work.

You can check how to decrease on page 91.

Cotton vest

You will need:
5(6) x 50g balls
double knitting
cotton

1 pair size
4½ mm needles

1 stitch holder

a row counter

1 darning needle

Tension

19 sts and 30 rows = 10cm in ridge stitch pattern, using size 4½mm needles.

Size

To fit 81 (86)cm/32″(34″) chest. Figures in brackets are for the larger size.

Front

Cast on 76(80)sts and work 6 rows in garter st. Then work in ridge pattern, as follows:
Row 1 Knit
Row 2 Purl
Row 3 Knit
Row 4 Knit
Repeat these 4 rows until you have worked 19(21) ridges.

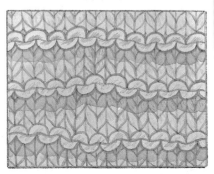

Shaping the armholes

Continuing in ridge pattern, cast off 6 sts at beginning of next 2 rows – 64(68) sts, then k2tog at each end of every row until there are 48(52 sts) left, ending with a p row.
Cont straight for 21(25) rows, but from now on knit the first and last 4 sts on every purl row to make garter st edges. *

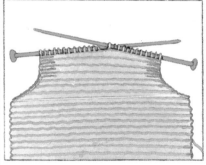

Neck shaping

Next row (row 4 of pattern)
Knit 18(19), then slip these sts on to a stitch holder. Cast off 12(14 sts), then knit the remaining 18(19) sts.

Left shoulder

Shape the left shoulder on the remaining 18(19) sts, as follows:
Row 1 K16(17), k2tog.
Row 2 K4, p9(10), k4.
Row 3 K15(16), k2tog.
Row 4, 8, 12 Knit.
Row 5 K14(15), k2tog.
Row 6 K4, p7(8), k4.
Row 7 K13(14), k2tog.
Row 9 K12(13), k2tog.
Row 10 K4, p5(6), k4.
Row 11 K11(12), k2tog.
Row 13 K10(11), k2tog.
Row 14 K4, p3(4), k4.
Row 15 K9(10), k2tog (10, 11 sts).

Cont straight in garter st for 16 rows. Cast off.

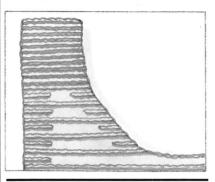

Right shoulder

Rejoin yarn to remaining 18(19) sts. Starting on right side, knit as for left shoulder but reverse the shaping by decreasing (k2tog) at the beginning, not the end, of every right side row.

Back

Work as for Front as far as *, then cont straight in pattern for another 8 rows before starting to shape neck. When neck shaping is finished, only work 8 rows garter st at top of shoulder.

Making up

Sew in the loose ends. Pin the side seams right sides together, matching the ridges. Backstitch neatly. Flat seam shoulder

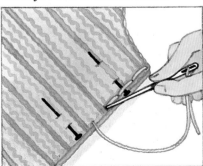

straps together. Press seams lightly on wrong side.

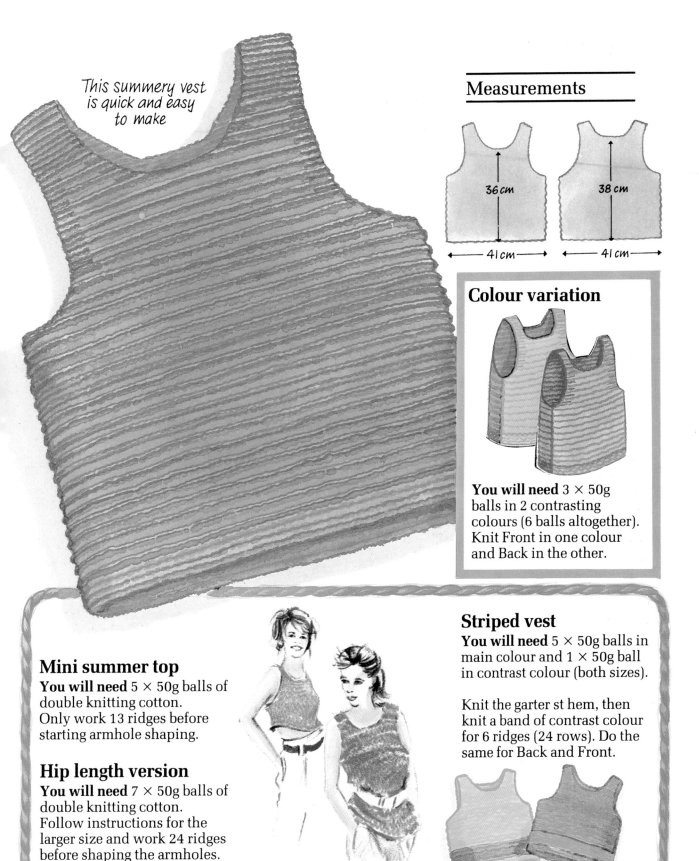

This summery vest is quick and easy to make

Measurements

36 cm

38 cm

41 cm

41 cm

Colour variation

You will need 3 × 50g balls in 2 contrasting colours (6 balls altogether). Knit Front in one colour and Back in the other.

Mini summer top

You will need 5 × 50g balls of double knitting cotton. Only work 13 ridges before starting armhole shaping.

Hip length version

You will need 7 × 50g balls of double knitting cotton. Follow instructions for the larger size and work 24 ridges before shaping the armholes.

Striped vest

You will need 5 × 50g balls in main colour and 1 × 50g ball in contrast colour (both sizes).

Knit the garter st hem, then knit a band of contrast colour for 6 ridges (24 rows). Do the same for Back and Front.

Tube skirt

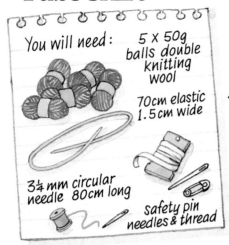

You will need: 5 x 50g balls double knitting wool

70cm elastic 1.5cm wide

3¼ mm circular needle 80cm long

safety pin needles & thread

Measurements

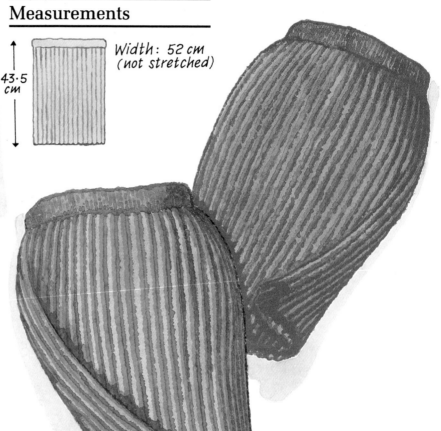

43.5 cm

Width: 52 cm (not stretched)

Knitting in the round

This skirt is knitted on a circular needle, so it does not have a seam. To knit in the round, you use a long, bendy double-ended needle. You cast on, then just keep knitting in the same direction, with the right side facing you.

Size

One size to fit hip size 88cm (34½ inches)

Method

Cast on 200 sts, using the ends of the circular needle as a pair. Tie a piece of coloured thread round the wool after the last st, to make a marker.

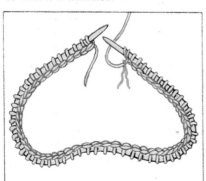

Start working in k2, p2 rib. To start the first row, knit the first stitch as shown, pulling the yarn tightly so there is no gap where the tube is joined.

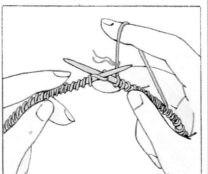

At the end of the row, carry straight on round to start the 2nd row. Cont in rib until work measures 40cm from beg, ending in line above the marker.

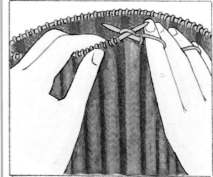

Decrease row

Next row Continuing in rib, decrease 1 st every 5 sts all along the row (knit 2 together or purl 2 together, depending on which type of stitch comes first) – you should have 160 sts left at the end of the row.

Waistband

Knit every row for 6cm. As you are knitting in the round, this will look like stocking stitch. Make sure you finish the last row in line with the marker, then cast off loosely.

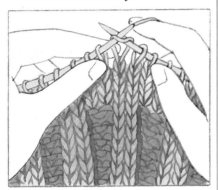

Making up

Fold waistband in half to wrong side of knitting and oversew the cast off edge to the decrease row, as shown, to make a casing. Leave a 4cm opening for the elastic.

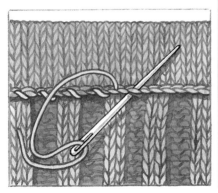

Fasten the safety pin to one end of the elastic and thread it through the waist casing, being careful not to twist it.

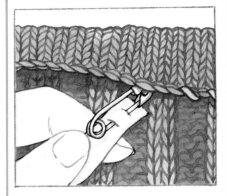

Pin the ends of the elastic together, then try the skirt on and adjust the elastic to fit your waist comfortably. Sew the ends of the elastic together firmly. Oversew the opening left in the waistband.

Long skirt

You will need 8 × 50g balls double knitting wool.

Knit as for short skirt, only knit 60cm of ribbing before the decrease row.

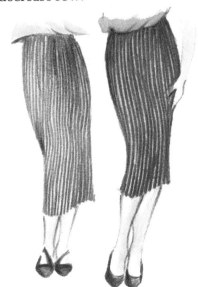

Striped skirts

Short version

You will need
1 × 50g balls in 5 colours
or
3 × 50g balls in 2 colours

Long version

You will need
1 × 50g ball in 8 colours
or
4 × 50g balls in 2 colours

Knit as for basic pattern, but knit 10cm stripes, using either 2 colours alternately or by making each stripe a different colour. Change the colours exactly in line with the hem marker thread each time, as the join will show slightly and should be straight. Darn in the loose ends before finishing.

Pink sweater

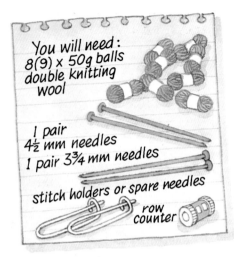

You will need:
8(9) x 50g balls
double knitting
wool

1 pair
4½ mm needles
1 pair 3¾ mm needles

stitch holders or spare needles

row counter

Tension

21 sts and 29 rows = 10cm in st st using 4½mm needles.

Size

To fit 81(86)cm/32(34) inch chest

Back

With size 3¾mm needles cast on 85(90) sts and work in k1, p1 rib for 7cm.
Next row Increase into 1st st, then every 12th st along the row, 92(98) sts. Change to size 4½mm needles and work in st st for 33(35)cm, ending with a purl row. Mark each end of the row with a thread. (To show where to position the sleeves when you sew them in later.)

Armhole shaping

Cast off 2 sts at beginning of next 2 rows, then decrease 1 st at each end of every knit row until there are 26 sts left. Leave these sts on a spare needle.

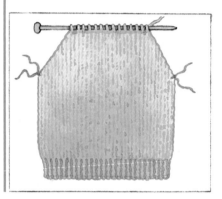

The pattern for this raglan sleeve sweater starts on this page and on the next few pages you will find lots of interesting ways to adapt the basic pattern.

Baggy mohair

Letter on front

Striped

Front

Work as for Back, including armhole shaping, until 47 sts left. Finish with a purl row.

Neck shaping

K2tog, k14 and slip the rest of the sts on to a stitch holder. Work left side of neck on remaining 15 sts, as follows:
Row 1 P2tog, p to end.
Row 2 K2tog, k to last 2 sts, k2 tog.
Repeat these 2 rows once.
Row 5 P2tog, p to end – 8 sts.
Continue decreasing at armhole edge on every k row until there is 1 st left. Cast off.

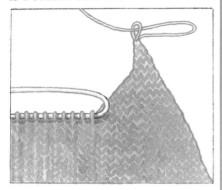

Leave middle 14(15) sts on stitch holder. Slip remaining 16 sts on to a needle. With right side of work facing you, rejoin wool to the sts on the needle. Knit as far as last 2 sts, k2tog.

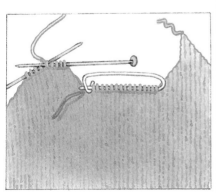

Work right side of neck as follows:
Row 1 P to last 2 sts, p2tog.
Row 2 K2tog, k to last 2 sts, k2tog.
Repeat these 2 rows once.
Row 5 P to last 2 sts, p2tog.
Continue decreasing at armhole edge on every k row until there is 1 st left. Cast off.

Sleeves

With size 3¾mm needles cast on 37(41) sts and work in k1, p1 rib for 15cm.
Next row Increase into 1st st and every 4th st after that – 46(52) sts.
Change to size 4½mm needles and cont in st st. Increase 1 st at each end of every 8th row until there are 69(74) sts. Cont straight until work measures 50(53)cm from beg, ending with a purl row.

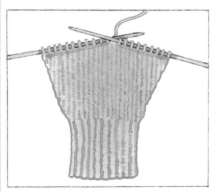

Armhole shaping

Cast off 2 sts at beg of next 2 rows, then dec 1 st at each end of every 4th row until there are 59(61) sts left. Then dec at each end of every k row until there are 7 sts left. Put these on a spare needle or stitch holder.

Knit the second sleeve in exactly the same way.

Measurements

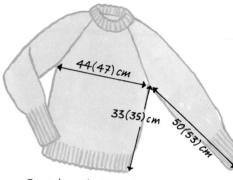

44(47) cm

33(35) cm

50(53) cm

Back length : 58 (61) cm

Things to remember

To increase

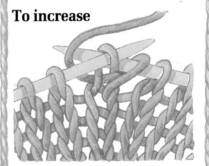

Knit twice into the same stitch (see p.90). At the end of a row, knit twice into the 2nd to last stitch.

To decrease

Knit two stitches together on a knit row, and purl two stitches together on a purl row (see p.91)

Pink sweater 2

Neckband

With the right side of the knitting facing you, pick up the stitches round the neck with a size 3¾mm needle. Knit the 26 stitches left at the top of the Back.

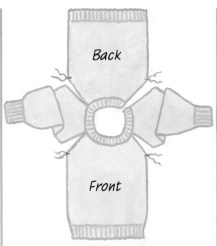

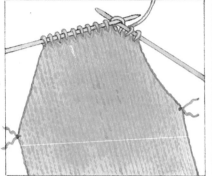

Knit the 7 sts at the top of one sleeve, then pick up 14 sts down the side of the Front neck, as shown at bottom of page. Knit the centre 14(15) sts of the neck, pick up the 14 sts back to the shoulder and knit across the 7 sts at the top of second sleeve. You should have 82(83) sts altogether. Knit 6cm of k1, p1 rib and leave the sts on the needle.

Sewing the neckband

Turn the knitting inside out. Thread a length of yarn on to a darning needle and make a couple of firm stitches at the base of the neckband.

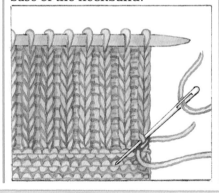

Fold the neckband in half, to the wrong side of the knitting, and loosely sew each stitch from the needle in turn to the first row of the ribbing.

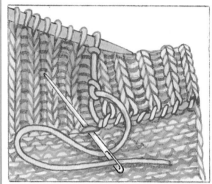

By sewing the neckband down like this you get a firm but stretchy neckband that you can pull over your head easily.

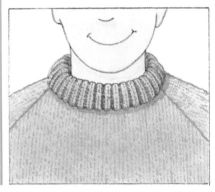

How to pick up stitches along an edge

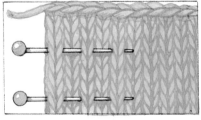

When you pick up new stitches, try to space them evenly or the edge will pucker. Aim to pick up 3 stitches out of every 4 row ends.

Hold the knitting in your left hand and the needle and yarn in your right hand. Put the needle between the lst and 2nd sts in from the edge.

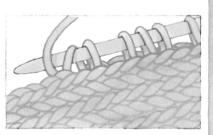

Wind the yarn round the needle, as if doing a knit stitch, and pull the loop through to make a new stitch. Repeat along the edge.

"Blocking" the knitting

Before you press a sweater, it is a good idea to shape it by pinning each piece in turn out to the right size. Knitters call this 'blocking'. It may seem fiddly, but it is well worth the trouble as you will find it easier to sew up your knitting and the finished result will look very professional. Remember to sew in all the loose yarn ends before you press your knitting.

To block knitting you need a firm, padded surface, so cover a table with a folded blanket or thick towels.

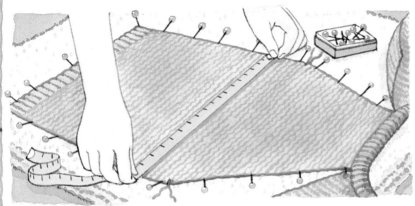

Lay the knitting, right side down, on top and smooth each piece out to the measurements given in the pattern and pin the edges down, as shown. Be careful not to stretch the knitting and make sure the rows run in straight lines.

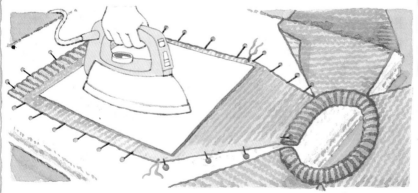

Gently press the knitting, a bit at a time, using a damp cloth and warm iron. Only press the stocking stitch areas, not the ribbing*. Leave the knitting on the table until it has cooled and dried, then you can take out the pins.

Sewing up the sweater

Pin the sleeves into the armholes, right sides together, above the marker threads and backstitch the shoulder seams.

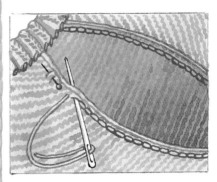

Backstitch the underarm sleeve seams and side seams as far as the cuff and hem ribbing. Flat seam the cuffs and ribbing.

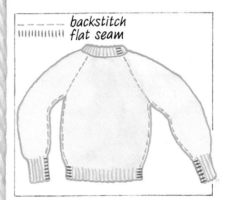

Flat seam the ends of the neckband together. Press the seams lightly and fold the cuffs back on the right side.

---

*See page 92 for how to press knitting and page 93 on ways of sewing up seams.

Striped sweater

You can knit the basic sweater in stripes. Here are some ideas for different types of stripe and you can find more on page 67. It is best to keep stripes simple and knit them all the same width. Knit a sample before you start, to check that the colours you have chosen go well together, and write down how many rows there are in each colour.

Joining new colours

If you are knitting narrow stripes in 2 or 3 colours you can carry a colour you are not using loosely up the side of the knitting until needed, then twist it round the previous colour before you start the new row.

For wide stripes, break off the wool and join the new colour as you would a new ball of wool (see page 64).

Yarn quantities

If you are using 2 colours in equal stripes you will need 2 × 50g balls of the ribbing colour + 4 × 50g balls in each of the 2 colours for the stripes.

For narrow stripes on a background colour you will need 7 × 50g balls in the main colour (including ribbing) and 2 × 50g balls in the contrast colours.

You can use up leftover wool as long as it is all the same type of wool and you have enough. Weigh it and check that you have at least 450g.

Matching stripes

Narrow stripes

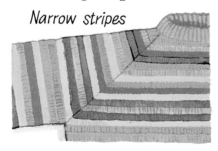

Make sure that the stripes match on the body and sleeves by starting the raglan shaping on the sleeves and the body on the same colour stripe.

Wide stripes

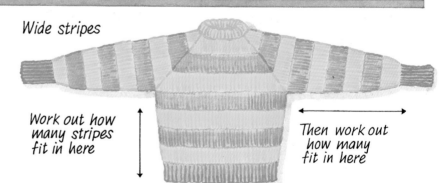

Work out how many stripes fit in here

Then work out how many fit in here

Decide how wide to make the stripes and work out from the pattern measurements how many will fit between the ribbing and armholes on the Back and Front. Then work out from the armhole down how many stripes will fit on the sleeves. Write down how many stripes there are on each piece.

Baggy square sweater

You can knit this loose, boxy sweater by following the basic sweater pattern and leaving out the ribbing. The edges of the sweater will roll outwards slightly as you wear it and cover the cast-on and cast-off stitches. The chest and length measurements will be the same as for the basic sweater.

You will need 9 × 50g balls of double knitting wool and a pair of size 4½mm needles.

Back and Front

Follow the instructions for the larger size sweater, but do not knit the ribbing. Cast on 97 stitches for the front and back, then work in stocking stitch, following the pattern from the top of the ribbing onwards. You will need to knit 42cm up to the beginning of the armhole shaping, as there is no ribbing. Cast off the stitches at the top of the Back and Front.

Sleeves

Cast on 50 stitches, then follow the pattern instructions from the beginning of the stocking stitch onwards. Cast off the stitches left at the top of the sleeves.

Making up

Do not knit a neckband. Press each piece of knitting carefully (see page 92). Backstitch the sleeves into the armholes, as in the basic pattern, then backstitch the underarm and side seams.

You can wear this sweater with the tube skirt on p.70

Contrasting sleeves

To knit this sweater you will need 5 × 50g balls of wool for the body and 4 × 50g balls for two sleeves.

For this one you will need 5 × 50g balls for the body and 2 × 50g balls in two extra colours for each sleeve.

Picture knitting

You can knit a sweater with your initial or a number on it, following the basic sweater pattern on page 68. You will need the same amount of yarn plus one ball in a contrasting colour. Before you start the sweater, make a chart of the picture you want, showing which colour to knit each stitch. Patterns always use charts for multi-coloured knits, as they are easier to follow than written instructions.

Making a chart

You will need:
squared paper
ruler
coloured pencils
pencil or felt pen
your knitting pattern

Decide how big to make the motif, then work out how many stitches and rows it will take up, using the tension for the pattern as a guide. For example, a letter to fit a 10cm square will take up 21 sts and 29 rows. (A 20cm square will take up 42 sts and 58 rows).

On the squared paper draw a rectangle 21 squares across and 29 squares high. Each square represents a stitch and each line a row. Then draw your letter or number to fit in the rectangle. Keep the shape bold and step the curves to fit the grid. Then lightly colour it in.

Following a chart

From a chart you can see straightaway which colour to knit every stitch. Starting at the bottom you read from right to left for a knit row and from left to right for a purl row. Laying a ruler across the chart below the row you are knitting will help you to keep your place as you go along.

Chart for a number

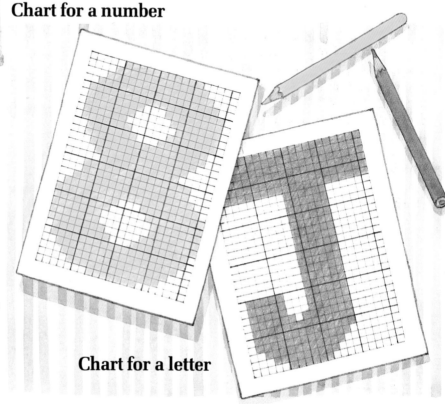

Chart for a letter

Where to put the motif

From the measurements of the sweater, decide where to put the motif. It is easiest to knit it before you start the armhole shaping. If you want the motif to be in the centre of the sweater, work out from the pattern how many stitches there should be on either side of it.

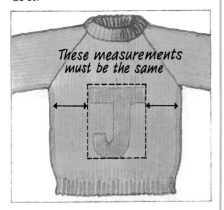

These measurements must be the same

Knitting the motif

For the letter J you need two balls of wool in the main colour and one in the contrasting colour.* Following the chart, knit as far as the first stitch of the motif in the main colour. Join the contrast colour, leaving a loose end, and knit the number of stitches shown on the chart. Then join the second ball of the main colour and knit to the end of the row.

On the following rows, change the balls of wool for different colour areas, but from now on cross the old colour over the new one when you knit a stitch in a new colour, as shown. This stops you from getting holes where the colours join. Be careful not to tangle the balls of wool.

On a knit row

On a purl row

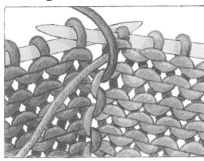

When you have finished the motif, break off the contrast yarn and the extra ends of the main colour. Sew these into the back of the knitting later.

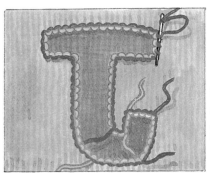

Other pictures

You can design and knit other motifs in the same way as long as you work them out on squared paper first.

Keep your designs simple and do not use too many colours in a row. You need a separate ball of wool for each colour change in any one row, so if there are two bands of contrast colour, wind a second ball from your ball of contrast wool.

* If your initial or number has two bands of contrast colour, wind a second ball from your ball of contrast colour.

Blue jacket

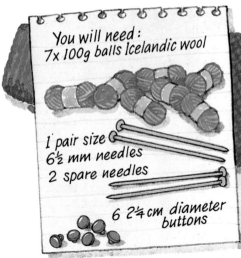

You will need:
7 x 100g balls Icelandic wool

1 pair size
6½ mm needles
2 spare needles

6 2¼ cm diameter buttons

This chunky jacket is made in moss stitch with garter stitch borders

Size

One size to fit 81-87cm (32"-34") chest.

Moss stitch

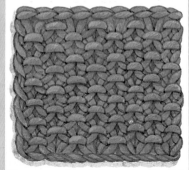

You can check how to do this on page 10. The tension is 14 sts and 24 rows to 10cm, using size 6½mm needles.

Back

With size 6½mm needles cast on 66 sts and knit 8 rows garter st (knit every row). Then change to moss st and continue until work measures 52cm from beginning. Cast off 21 sts at beginning of the next 2 rows and leave remaining 24 sts on a spare needle.

Pockets

Make 2 pockets. For each one cast on 14 sts and work 10cm in moss st. Leave both the pockets on spare needles.

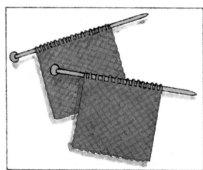

Left front

Cast on 36 sts and knit 8 rows garter st, then continue in moss st until work measures 13cm from beginning.

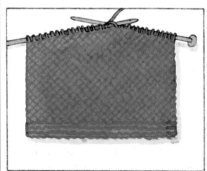

80

Adding the pocket

Continuing in moss st, work 5 sts, then cast off 14 sts. Knit the 14 sts at the top of one of the pockets, then continue to end of row (check that you have not made any mistakes in the moss st). Push the pocket flap to the wrong side of the knitting.

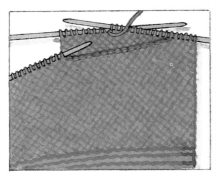

Continue straight until work measures 45cm from beginning.

Neck shaping

At beginning of next row on wrong side of knitting (the neck edge) cast off 7 sts. Continuing in moss st, decrease 1 st at neck edge on next 2 rows, then 1 st on every alternate row until there are 21 sts left.

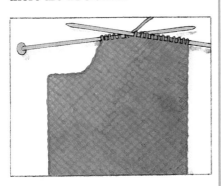

Continue straight until work measures 52cm from beginning. Cast off remaining sts loosely.

Right front

Cast on 36 sts and work 8 rows in garter st, then make the 1st buttonhole.

Making a buttonhole

Row 1 Work 3 sts in moss st, cast off 2 sts, then continue to end of row.
Row 2 Work 31 sts in moss st up to cast off sts, turn knitting, cast on 2 sts, turn knitting back and continue to end of row.

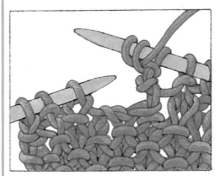

You have to make 6 buttonholes like this up the jacket front. Space them 8cm apart. The last buttonhole should come about 2cm before you start to shape the neck.

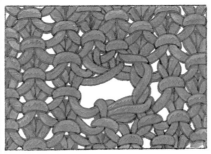

Continue straight, making buttonholes where needed, until you have knitted 13cm moss st, then knit in the pocket:
Next row Moss st 17, cast off 14 then knit the 14 at the top of the

pocket in moss st, and moss st to end of row. Continue straight until work measures 45cm from beginning, ending with a wrong side row.

Shape neck

Cast off 7 sts at beginning of next row, then continue in moss st, decreasing 1 st at neck edge on next 2 rows, then every alternate row until there are 21 sts left. Continue straight until work measures 52cm from beginning, then cast off loosely.

Sleeves

Cast on 30 sts. Work 8 rows in garter st, then continue in moss st. Increase* 1 st at each end of the row every 2cm until you have 64 sts. Continue straight until work measures 42cm. Work 8 rows of garter st, then cast off loosely.

Measurements

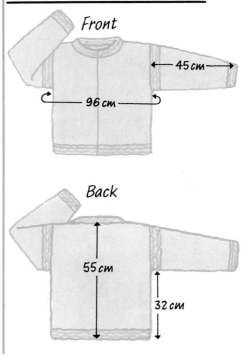

Front

45 cm

96 cm

Back

55 cm

32 cm

---

*You can check how to increase on page 90.

Blue jacket 2

Making up

Pin each piece of knitting out to the right measurements, right side down* and gently press it on the wrong side.

Sew up the shoulder seams with flat seams.

Neckband

Pick up the stitches for the neckband with the right side of the knitting facing you. Start at the neck edge of the right Front.

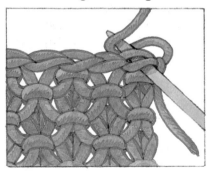

Pick up the 7 cast off sts, then 14 sts up to the shoulder, spacing them evenly**. Knit up the 24 sts at the top of the Back, then pick up 14 sts down the side of the left Front neck and the 7 cast off sts to the centre Front. You should have 66 sts altogether. Knit 4 rows garter st, then cast off loosely.

Pin the backs of the pockets flat against the wrong side of the Front pieces and oversew round the 3 free sides.

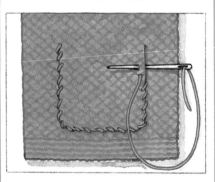

Measure 23cm down the Back and Front from the shoulder seams and sew in marker threads in a contrasting colour. Pin the sleeves into the armholes between the marker threads and sew them in with flat seams.

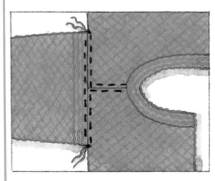

Matching underarm seams, flat seam sleeve and side seams and press seams lightly.

Buttons

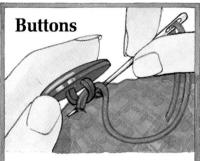

Plain buttons look best on this jacket. They can be in a matching or contrasting colour. Buttons with a shank are best for chunky knits like this.

Positioning the buttons

You must sew the buttons in the right place and in a straight line, or they will spoil the look of the jacket. Lay the buttonhole edge of the jacket over the edge of the left front by about 4cm, so the buttonholes cover the edge. Make sure the top and bottom edges of the jacket match and keep the buttonhole edge straight. Mark where the centre of each buttonhole comes with a pin, to show where to sew on the buttons.

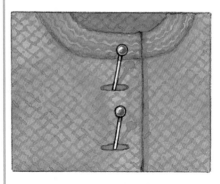

When you have sewn on the buttons, check that they are in the right place. They should be about 2cm in from the edge of the jacket.

Zip-up jacket

Jacket with collar and zip down the front

Instead of buttons you will need an open-ended zip the same length as the finished Front (approximately 45cm). It is better to buy a zip that is slightly too short rather than one which is too long, so you can ease it into place without stretching the edges of the knitting.

Follow the basic pattern for the jacket, only leave out the buttonholes on the right Front. To add a collar to the jacket, knit 10cm garter st instead of 8 rows for the neckband, then fold it over.

Sewing in the zip

Keep the zip closed and pin it to the wrong side of the Front opening. The edges of the knitting should be very close to the teeth and the right and left Front should match at the top and bottom.

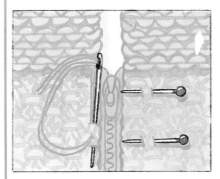

Using a sewing needle and a double strand of sewing thread in a matching colour, backstitch one side of the zip firmly in place. Start at the top and work down to the bottom, sewing about 2 sts in from the edge of the jacket. Do the same on the other side. Turn the jacket inside out, tuck in the top ends of the zip and sew them down.

Different yarns

You can knit this jacket in other types of chunky wool, as long as the yarn labels recommend the same size needles. Check the tension before you start, to make sure the jacket ends up the right size.

You could also knit it in a mohair that recommends the same needle size. Mohair should be knitted loosely and you must not press it.

Aran sweater

This sweater looks complicated but it is quite easy. You can make it with either a polo neck or a crew neck.

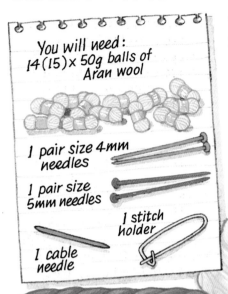

You will need:
14 (15) x 50g balls of Aran wool

1 pair size 4mm needles

1 pair size 5mm needles

1 stitch holder

1 cable needle

Aran knitting

Aran sweaters have a very patterned surface with cables and several different types of stitch on them. They were first knitted in the Aran islands, off the coast of Ireland, by the wives of the fishermen. Each type of stitch or cable had its own meaning and the women made up their own patterns.

Traditionally the sweaters are knitted in natural coloured wool, like the sweater here.

Tension

18 sts and 24 rows = 10cm in dbl moss st, using 5mm needles.

Size

One size to fit 81-87cm (32-34 inch) chest.

Measurements

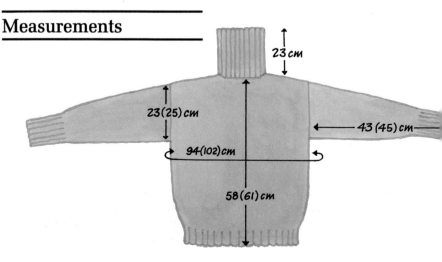

23 cm

23 (25) cm

43 (45) cm

94 (102) cm

58 (61) cm

There are only three different kinds of stitch used in this pattern: ribbing, double moss stitch and cables.

You can find out how to do double moss stitch and cables for the sweater on this page, and the pattern starts on the next page.

Double moss stitch

Row 1 k2, p2 to last 2 sts, k2.
Row 2 p2, k2 to last 2 sts, p2.
Row 3 p2, k2 to last 2 sts, p2.
Row 4 k2, p2 to last 2 sts, k2.
Rep these 4 rows throughout.

What does m1 mean?

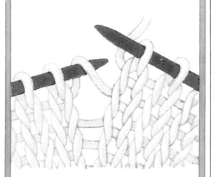

For Row 1, where it says m1, it means make a new stitch by increasing between the stitches. You can find out how to do this on p.90.

Knitting cables

When you knit a cable, you cross one group of stitches first over, then behind, another group of stitches. You use a cable needle to hold the first group of stitches out of the way until you want to knit them. Always use a cable needle the same size or smaller than the other needles you are using so it does not stretch the stitches.

In this pattern there are cables 4 stitches wide and 8 stitches wide. They are both knitted in the same way; you just slip more stitches on to the cable needle to make the wider cable. Here you can find out how to knit a cable 4 stitches wide.

Cable that twists to the left

1

2

Slip 2 stitches on to the cable needle and hold them at the front of the knitting, then knit the next 2 stitches.

Now knit the 2 stitches from the cable needle.

Cable that twists to the right

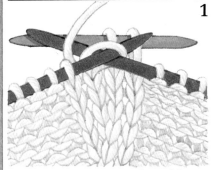

1

2

Slip 2 stitches on to the cable needle and hold them at the back of the knitting, then knit the next 2 stitches.

Now knit the 2 stitches from the cable needle.

Aran sweater 2

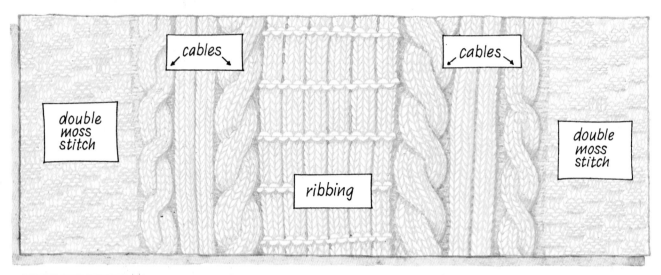

double moss stitch

cables

cables

double moss stitch

ribbing

Back

Cast on 80(86) sts on size 4mm needles and work k2, p2 rib for 7cm.

Increase row Rib 8(7), m1 * rib 4, m1 ** to the last 8(7) sts, rib to the end of the row – 97(105) sts.

Change to size 5mm needles and start the Aran pattern as follows. The pattern has 16 rows which you keep repeating. By the time you have knitted them once, you will find it much easier to follow.

Aran pattern

Row 1 Double moss st 14(18), p2, k4, p2, k2, p2, k2, p2, k8, p2, (k2, p1) 5 times, k2, p2, k8, p2, k2, p2, k2, p2, k4, p2, double moss st 14(18).

Row 2 Double moss st 14(18), k2, p4, k2, p2, k2, p2, k2, p8, k2, (p2, k1) 5 times, p2, k2, p8, k2, p2, k2, p2, p4, k2, double moss st 14(18).

Row 3 Repeat row 1.

Row 4 Repeat row 2.

Row 5 Double moss st 14(18), p2, slip 2 sts on to cable needle at front of work, k2, k2 sts from cable needle, p2, k2, p2, k2, p2, k8, p2, (k2, p1) 5 times, k2, p2, k8, p2, k2, p2, k2, p2, slip 2 sts on to cable needle at back of work, k2, k2 sts from cable needle, p2, double moss st 14(18).

Row 6 Repeat row 2.

Row 7 Double moss st 14 (18), p2, k4, p2, k2, p2, k2, p2, slip 4 sts on to cable needle at front of work, k4, k4 sts from cable needle, p21, slip 4 sts on to cable needle at back of work, k4, k4 sts from cable needle, p2, k2, p2, k2, p2, k4, p2, double moss st 14(18).

Row 8 Repeat row 2.
Row 9 Repeat row 3.
Row 10 Repeat row 2.
Row 11 Repeat row 3.
Row 12 Repeat row 2.
Row 13 Repeat row 5.

Row 14 Repeat row 2.
Row 15 Repeat row 7.
Row 16 Repeat row 2.

Repeat the 16 rows of pattern until knitting measures 58(61)cm from beginning.

Shaping shoulders

Next row Cast off 32(36) sts at beginning of row, slip next 33 sts on to a stitch holder, cast off last 32(36)sts.

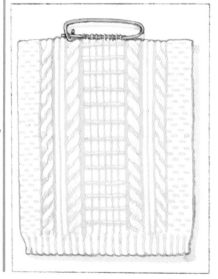

Front

Repeat as for Back until work measures 47 (54)cm from beginning.

Shaping the neck

Work 40(43)sts in Aran pattern and slip rest of stitches on to a stitch holder. Continue left shoulder in pattern on the stitches already knitted, decreasing 1st at beginning of every wrong side row until there are 32 (36) sts left.

Continue straight in pattern until work measures 58(61)cm, then cast off loosely.

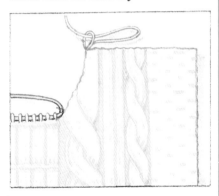

Leave centre 17 sts on a stitch holder and knit right shoulder on remaining sts. Continuing in pattern, cast off 1 st at the beginning of right side rows until there are 32(36) sts left. Continue as for left shoulder.

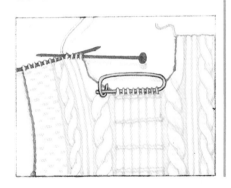

Sleeves

Cast on 36(38) sts on size 4mm needles and work k2, p2 rib for 14cm.

Next row Increase 24(26) sts as follows: (k1, m1), k1, m1, k1, m1, k1, * k1, m1, k1, m1, k2, m1, k2, m1 **, repeat from * to ** to the last 3(4) sts, (k1, m1), k1, m1, k1.

Row 1 (K2), p2, k4, p2, k2, p2, k2, p2, k8, p2, k2, p1, k2, p1, k2, p2, k8, p2, k2, p2, k2, p2, k4, p2, (k2).

Row 2 (P2), k2, p4, k2, p2, k2, p2, k2, p8, k2, p2, k1, p2, k1, p2, k2, p8, k2, p2, k2, p2, k2, p4, k2, (p2).

Row 3 (K2), p2, k4, p2, k2, p2, k2, p2, k8, p2, k2, p1, k2, p1, k2, p2, k8, p2, k2, p2, k2, p2, k4, p2, (k2).

Row 4 Repeat row 2.

Row 5 (K2), p2, slip 2 sts on to cable needle at front of work, k2, k2 sts from cable needle, p2, k2, p2, k2, p2, k8, p2, k2, p1, k2, p1, k2, p2, k8, p2, k2, p2, k2, p2, slip 2 sts on to cable needle at back of work, k2, k2 sts from cable needle, p2 (k2).

Row 6 Repeat row 2.

Row 7 (k2), p2, k4, p2, k2, p2, k2, p2, slip 4 sts on to cable needle at front of work, k4, k4 sts from cable needle, p12, slip 4 sts on to cable needle at back of work, k4, k4 sts from cable needle, p2, k2, p2, k2, p2, k4, p2(k2).

Row 8 Repeat row 2.
Row 9 Repeat row 3.

Row 10 Repeat row 2.
Row 11 Repeat row 3.
Row 12 Repeat row 2.
Row 13 Repeat row 5.
Row 14 Repeat row 2.
Row 15 Repeat row 7.
Row 16 Repeat row 2.

Following Aran pattern, increase 1 st at each end of a right side row every 2.5cm until there are 86 (92)sts. Knit the new sts in double moss st. When you have finished increasing, you should have 14(17)sts in double moss st on each side of the sleeve. Continue straight until work measures 50(52)cm from beginning. Cast off.

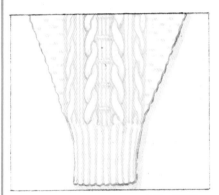

Keeping your place

Use a row counter and mark where you are up to on the pattern, so that you do not lose your place.

Aran sweater 3

Polo neck

You knit the neck for this sweater before you sew it up, as for the pink sweater on page 72. This makes it easier to sew up the sweater.

With the right side of the work facing you, pick up the stitches for the neck with a size 4mm needle. You can find out how to do this at the bottom of page 74. Knit across the 33 sts at the top of the Back, then pick up 18 sts down the left side of Front neck, 17 sts across the centre of the neck and 18 sts up the right side of neck. You should have 86 sts altogether.

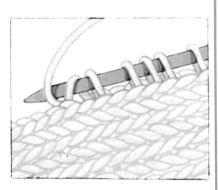

With size 4mm needles, work k2, p2 rib for 23cm. Cast off.

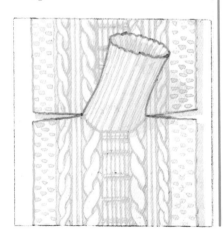

Pressing

Pin each piece of knitting in turn out to the correct size, right side down (see page 75). Lightly press the pieces on the wrong side (but do not press the ribbing).

Making up

Measure 23(25)cm down from the shoulders and make tacks in coloured thread to show where to sew in the sleeves.

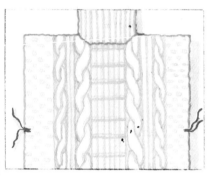

Lay the Back and Front right sides together and backstitch the shoulder seams. Open the sweater out and pin and backstitch the sleeves in place between the tacks.

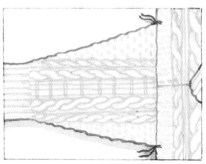

Backstitch the sleeve underarm seams and the side seams as far as the cuffs and ribbing. Sew up the cuffs, ribbing and polo neck with flat seams. Fold the cuffs back and the polo neck down.

Crew neck sweater

To knit a ribbed crew neck instead of a polo neck, follow the instructions for picking up the neck sts, but only knit 6cm in k2, p2 rib. Leave the stitches on the needle, then fold the neckband in half to the wrong side of the knitting and loosely sew each stitch in turn to the first row of the neck ribbing. You can find out how to do this on page 74.

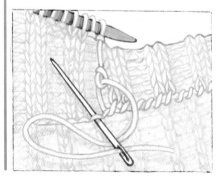

Making your knitting fit

Before you start knitting anything for yourself, take your measurements so that you know which size to knit. All the patterns in this book have been designed to fit sizes 10 and 12.

Below you can see which measurements you need to take for most knitting patterns. The chart to the right shows you the standard measurements for sizes 10 and 12.

Size chart

Metric			Imperial		
10		**12**	**10**		**12**
83cm	chest	87cm	32½″	chest	34″
64cm	waist	67cm	25″	waist	26½″
88cm	hips	92cm	34½″	hips	36″

Taking measurements

Chest

Length of back from nape of neck to waist

Under arm to wrist

What is ease?

Too tight

Too loose

Most knitting patterns are designed to allow some 'ease'. This means that the garment is not skin tight, but allows room for movement. For example a sweater for someone with a size 32″ chest will actually measure 34″ around the chest.

Altering the length

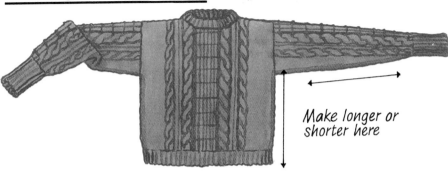

Make longer or shorter here

If you want your sweater to be longer or shorter than it says in the pattern, work out what measurement you want it to be up to the armhole and alter the length before shaping the armhole. You alter the length of sleeves in the same way.

Increasing stitches

Increasing and decreasing the number of stitches on your needles are ways of shaping your knitting. Knitting patterns always tell you when to increase or decrease, but not usually how to do it. On these two pages you can find out.

You usually only increase stitches on a knit row. There are two basic ways to do this.

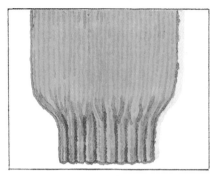

Where a pattern tells you to increase several stitches across a row, at the top of ribbing for example, it is best to increase between the stitches.

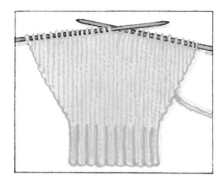

If the pattern tells you to increase at each end of a row, when knitting a sleeve for example, increase by knitting twice into the same stitch.

Increasing between stitches

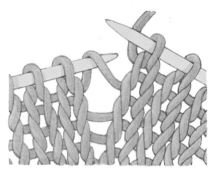

Pick up the thread between the two stitches on the row below with your left needle.

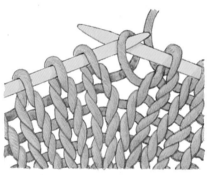

Now knit into the back of the loop. This twists the stitch so it does not make a hole.

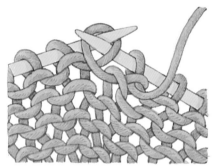

On a purl row, purl into the back of the loop, as shown.

Knitting twice into the same stitch

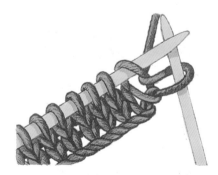

Knit into the stitch in the usual way, but do not slip it off the left needle.

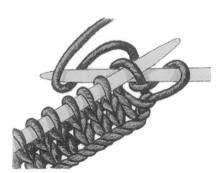

Then knit into the back of the same stitch, to make two stitches, and carry on as usual.

At the end of a row, knit twice into the second-to-last stitch, not the last one. This gives your knitting a more even edge.

How to decrease stitches

You decrease stitches to make knitting narrower, for example when shaping armholes. Patterns usually tell you to decrease one stitch at each end of a row. The easiest way to do this is to knit or purl two stitches together. Some people find it better not to include the first or last stitches in a row because this stitch can make the edge of the knitting uneven.

Knitting 2 stitches together

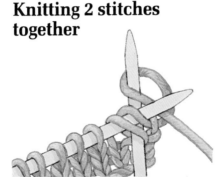

Put the right needle into two stitches, as shown, and knit them together as if they were one stitch.

Purling 2 stitches together

Put the right needle into two stitches, as shown, and purl them together as if they were one stitch.

Neat armholes

When you knit 2 stitches together, they slant either to the right or left. If you are shaping a raglan armhole it looks best if the stitches slant in the same direction as the edge of the knitting.

Knitting or purling stitches together on the right side of stocking stitch makes them slant to the right. To make stitches slant to the left, knit them together through the back of the stitches.

Knitting stitches together through the back of the stitches

Put the right needle through the back loops of two stitches, as shown, and knit them together.

Purling stitches together through the back of the stitches

Put the right needle through the backs of two stitches, as shown, and purl them together.

Making the stitches slant the right way

decrease edge

decrease edge

On a knit row, k2 tog through the back of the stitches at the beginning of the row and k2 tog at the end of the row.

On a purl row, p2 tog at the beginning of the row and p2 tog through the back of the stitches at the end of the row.

Finishing off your knitting

To make your knitting look professional, you must finish it off carefully.

You will need:
iron
pressing cloth
darning needle
pins
leftover yarn
tape measure

How to measure your knitting

Measure your knitting as you do it, to make sure each piece is the right size, or you will have problems sewing it up.

Lay the knitting flat on a table or the floor, making sure you do not stretch it. Measure straight up the middle of it, not up one of the edges.

Pressing

Pressing knitting makes it look more even and 'finished'. Only press your knitting if the pattern tells you to, as many synthetic yarns should not be pressed at all. Check the yarn label too, just to make sure. On the chart below you can see what the different ironing symbols mean.

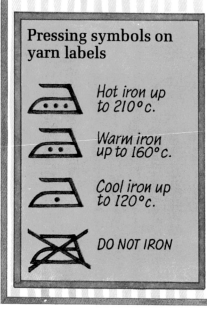

Pressing Guide

Pressing symbols on yarn labels

Hot iron up to 210°c.

Warm iron up to 160°c.

Cool iron up to 120°c.

DO NOT IRON

Pure wool Press under a damp cloth with a warm iron.

Cotton Press under a damp cloth with a warm iron.

Do not press

Most synthetic yarns and blends. Always check what the yarn label says.

Ribbing Pressing ribbing flattens it out and makes it lose its stretchiness

Deeply patterned knitting. Pressing can flatten the pattern.

Turn the iron on to the right temperature. Always press knitting on the wrong side, so lay it, right side down, on the ironing board. Cover the knitting with a damp cloth. Gently lay the iron on it for a few seconds, then lift it up.

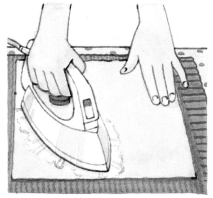

Do not move the iron around as you usually do. Press all of the knitting evenly in this way, a bit at a time. Try not to press so hard that you flatten the knitting. Let it dry properly, then sew it up.

Sewing up your knitting

Knitting patterns always tell you in what order to sew up your knitting. The patterns in this book also tell you what kind of seam to use. The most useful types of seam are the flat seam and the backstitch seam.

Sew up seams with the knitting yarn and a tapestry or darning needle. If your yarn is very thick, use a 4 ply yarn the same colour instead.

Sewing in yarn ends

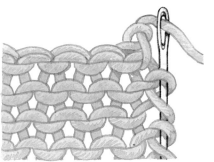

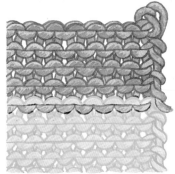

Thread each loose end in turn on to a darning needle and sew it neatly into a seam or the back of the knitting, to hold it firm.

Trim any extra yarn close to the knitting. If you have used more than one colour, sew each loose end into its own colour area.

Backstitch

Backstitch can be used for most seams but it makes a ridge and should not be used for ribbing.

Pin the two pieces right sides together, matching the row ends if possible. Start off with a couple of small stiches, one on top of the other, then sew the seam as shown, from right to left. Sew in the yarn firmly at the end of the seam with a couple of small stitches.

1

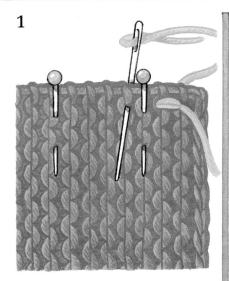

Flat seaming

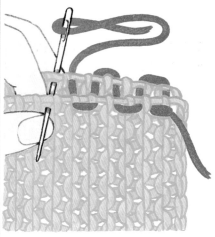

Use this for sewing up ribbing and things you have knitted with thick yarn.

Put the knitting right sides together, matching the rows if you are sewing up a straight edge. Put your left forefinger between the two pieces of knitting and join the yarn with a couple of stitches. Sew the seam, as shown, being careful not to sew too tightly. Finish it off as for backstitch.

2

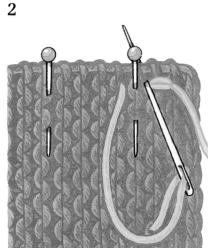

3

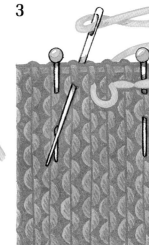

Putting mistakes right

Unfortunately when you knit, things go wrong from time to time. Do not despair. It is easy to put mistakes right and does not take long.

Every knitter drops a stitch from time to time. Here you can find out how to pick up dropped stitches on both knit and purl rows.

Picking up a dropped knit stitch

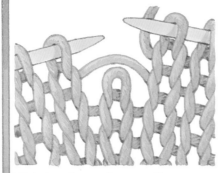

This is what a dropped knit stitch looks like.

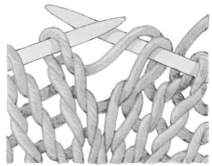

Pick up both the dropped stitch and the loop above it with your right needle, as shown.

Picking up a dropped purl stitch

This is what a dropped purl stitch looks like.

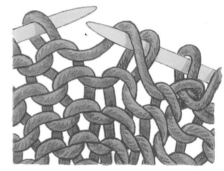

Use your right needle to pick up both the dropped stitch and the loop above it, as shown.

Ladders

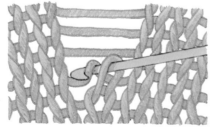

If you leave a dropped stitch, it unravels for several rows and makes a ladder. The easiest way to put this right is to pick up the stitches with a crochet hook.

On a knit row

Put the crochet hook through the front of the dropped stitch. Hook up the loop above it and pull it through the stitch to make a new stitch. Carry on like this to the top of the ladder.

On a purl row

Put the crochet hook through the back of the dropped stitch. Hook up a loop and pull it through the stitch to make a new one. Put the hook in again to make each new stitch.

Put the tip of your left needle from back to front into the stitch only.

Lift it over the loop and off the needle, to make a new stitch on the right needle.

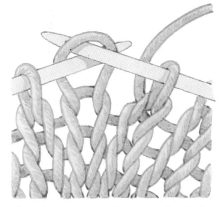

Slip the new stitch on to the left needle, so it is the right way round, as shown.

Put the tip of your left needle from front to back into the stitch only.

Lift the stitch over the loop so that you have a new stitch on the right needle.

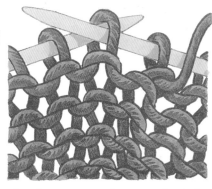

Slip the new stitch on to the left needle, as shown.

Unpicking mistakes

Knit stitches

Purl stitches

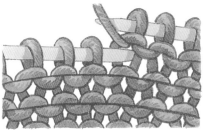

If you have made a mistake further back in a row, do not pull the knitting off the needles. Unpick one stitch at a time until you reach the mistake.

Put the left needle into the stitch below the 1st stitch on the right needle and drop the 1st stitch off the right needle. Repeat along the row, keeping the yarn at the back of the work.

Put the left needle purlwise into the stitch below the lst stitch on the right needle and drop the 1st stitch off the right needle. Repeat along the row, keeping the yarn to the front.

Index

abbreviations, 60
ankle warmers, 62
appliqué letter, 14
appliqué tee-shirt, 18
Aran sweater, 84-88, 92
asterisks, 60

backstitch, 93
baggy top, 22
bias binding, 17
blocking, 75, 82
bobbin, threading a, 4-5
bobble, woollen, making a, 67
buttonholes,
    handsewn, 43
    knitted, 81
    machine-stitched, 31
    position, 7, 82

cable needles, 54, 85
cable patterns, 84, 88
casing, sewn, 26
casting off, 58-59
casting on, 56-57
checks, 8
circular knitting needles, 54, 70
collar, sewn, 34
    knitted, 83
colour charts, 78-79
constructions marks, 6-7, 9
crew neck, 74, 88
crutch seam, 25
cuffs, ribbed sweatshirt, 22-23
    shirt, 35
cutting out, 8-9

darts, 7, 11
decreasing, 73, 91
dots, 7
double moss st, 85-88
double topstitching, 24
dropped stitches, 59, 94-95
dye lots, 53

ease, in sewing, 46
    in knitting, 89

fabrics, 44-45
    widths, 47
facings, 33, 39
flat seam, 93

garter stitch, 58
gathering, 29
gathered skirt, 28-31
grainline, 7, 9

haberdashery, 3
handsewing, 42-43
hat, bobble, 66-67

hems,
    machined, 13
    making a, 43
    marking a, 30

increasing, 73, 90
initial, how to knit an, 78-79
ironing, 3-11
ironing symbols,
    sewing, 11
    knitting, 92

jacket, 80, 83
jeans, 24, 27
jersey, 44, 45
    how to sew, 12
joining yarn, 64, 76
jumpsuit, 38-41

lengthening dress patterns, 48

machine buttonholes, 31
machine stitches, 5
making up, 61
measurements,
    sewing, 46
    knitting, 60, 61, 89
measuring knitting, 92
mini-dress, 15
mini tee-shirt, 18
mini-vest, 69
mistakes,
    (in knitting), 94-95
mittens, 62-63
mohair, 52
moss stitch, 58, 80
motif, knitting a, 78-79

nap, 8, 45, 47
neatening seams, 10
neckbands,
    collar, sewn, 34
    crew, knitted, 74
    ribbed, sweatshirt, 23
needles,
    handsewing, 42
    knitting, 54
    machine, 5
    tapestry, 55, 93

oversewing, 42

pattern paper, 6
patterned fabrics, 45
patterns,
    knitting, following, 60
    sewing, layouts, 8
    making (sewing), 6-7
    shop (sewing), 47
picking up dropped stitches, 94-95

picking up stitches, 74, 88
pinning, 10
pleats, 32
plys, 53
pockets,
    knitted, 64-65, 80-81
    sewn, 12, 25, 29, 33, 39
pressing, 11
    symbols, 11, 92
presser foot, 5
purl, how to, 56-57, 58

raglan sleeve sweater, 72-75
raglan sleeves, 21
ribbing (jersey), 20-23
ribbing, knitted, 72-75
ridge stitch (knitting), 68
round, knitting in the, 70
row counter, 55

scale of patterns (sewing), 6
scarf, 64, 65
seam allowance, 10, 33
seamline, 7, 10
seams,
    (knitting), 93
    (sewing), 10-11
selvedges, 7, 8, 9, 45
sewing machines, 4-5
sewing up knitting, 93
shade chart, 53
shank buttons, 31
shaping knitting, 90-91
shirt, 32-37
short-sleeved sweatshirt, 22
shortening dress patterns, 48
size chart,
    knitting, 89
sewing, 46
sizes,
    knitting, 50, 60, 89
    sewing, 2, 6
skirt, knitted, 70, 71
    sewn, 28-31
sleeve opening, 35
sleeves, sewing in, 17, 21, 34
    types of, 21
stitches,
    handsewing, 42-43
    machine, 5
    picking up, 74
    types of (knitted), 58, 68, 80, 85
stitch holder, 55
stocking stitch, 58
stripes, matching,
    for knitting, 76
    for sewing, 8
synthetic fabrics, 44
synthetic thread, 44

synthetic yarns, 52, 92
sweatshirt, 20-23

tacking, 10, 42
tailor tacks, 6-7, 9
tee-shirt, 16-19
tension,
    knitting, 60, 61
    sewing, 5, 10
thread, 42, 44
threading a bobbin, 4
threading a machine, 4-5
topstitching, 12
    double, 24
tube skirt, 70, 71

unpicking mistakes,
    knitting, 95
    sewing, 48

variations,
    knitting, 51
vest,
    knitted, 68, 69
    sewn, 12-15
view, 47

waistband,
    elasticated, 26, 71
    knitted, 71
    interfaced, 30
warp threads, 45
weft threads, 45
wool, 52, 92

yarn, 52-53
    ends, sewing in, 93
    joining, 64
    labels, 53
yoke, 33

zigzag stitches, 5, 12, 14
zip foot, 29
zip, sewing in a,
    (knitting), 83
    (sewing), 29

The yarns used to make the clothes in part 2 were supplied by the Yarn Store, 8 Ganton Street, London W1.

First published in 1985 by Usborne Publishing Ltd,
83-85 Saffron Hill, London EC1N 8RT, England.
Copyright © 1991, 1985 Usborne Publishing Ltd.

Printed in Belgium.